CHILDREN DRAW AND TELL

An Introduction to the Projective Uses of Children's Human Figure Drawings

By Marvin Klepsch, Dip. Ed. Psych., Ed.D.

and Laura Logie, M.A.

BRUNNER/MAZEL, *A member of the Taylor & Francis Group*

Library of Congress Cataloging in Publication Data

Klepsch, Marvin.
    Children draw and tell.

    Bibliography: p.
    Includes index.
    1. Drawing, Psychology of. 2. Child
psychology. 3. Projective techniques.
    I. Logie, Laura, 1915-   . II. Title.
[DNLM: 1. Art. 2. Projective technics – In
infancy and childhood. 3. Child psychology.
WS 105.5.E8 K64c]
BF723.D7K56   155.4'18   82-1214
ISBN 0-87630-298-3 (cloth)   AACR2

ISBN 0-87630-306-8 (paper)

Published by

BRUNNER/MAZEL
A member of the Taylor & Francis Group
1900 Frost Road, Suite 101
Bristol, PA 19007
1-800-821-8312

MANUFACTURED IN THE UNITED STATES OF AMERICA

20 19 18 17 16 15 14 13 12 11

FOREWORD

Children's drawings, after long centuries of utter neglect, first became the object of serious attention during the latter years of the nineteenth century. Until then, the children themselves were regarded as defective adults. Man was the standard by which they were to be judged. At long last, they came to be seen as persons in their own right with thoughts, feelings, and bodies peculiarly their own. Heretofore, their scribbles and tadpoles and funny manikins had found their way routinely into the refuse. Even the childhood work of the great masters was not spared total destruction.

The first publication with actual reproductions of child art appeared in 1887. The writer, Corrado Ricci, was a renowned art critic endowed with remarkable insight into the psychological implications of human figure drawings. This publication heralded the appearance of numerous scholarly publications here and abroad, notably: Sully (1895), Partridge (1902), Kerschensteiner (1905), Levinstein (1905), Katzaroff (1909-10), Luquet (1913).

A major step forward occurred in 1926 with the publication by F. Goodenough of a system for evaluating intelligence from human figure drawings. This was subsequently extended and carefully standardized by Harris (1963; Harris and Roberts, 1972). HFDs are an item in many IQ tests, notably the Stanford-Binet, but the Goodenough-Harris procedure earned the title of test in its own right, where "test" is reserved for those methods that meet the demands required of standardized procedures.

Convinced that through graphic images a person expresses more than thought, clinicians have long studied drawings in a flexible way for clues that might confirm or suggest a diagnostic approach to emotional difficulties. And clinicians persist along this path even without solid support from research that utilizes the impersonal strictures of scientific investigation. The recognition accorded drawings as expressions of intellectual maturity has given rise to a wave of research aimed at establishing validity to their projective use.

Widespread use of Rorschach and other projective approaches (Szondi test, Koch's Baumtest, TAT, Buck's H-T-P), as well as a new look at human figure drawings for evidence of emotional traits, has revived interest in projectives. Machover's method of personality investigation (1949) gained wide acceptance among psychologists, as did the scoring system devised by Koppitz (1968) and, more recently Burns and Kaufman's kinetic family drawings (1970, 1972). Though theorists may remain skeptical, psychologists unremittingly persist in their efforts to measure and analyze.

The present volume surveys numerous studies and research projects that have, with varying success, sought to bring some measure of scientific certainty to assessment by introducing the methods of statistical analysis and validation into the elusive realm of personality. In addition, the authors present the fruits of their own investigations with Indian children.

The volume is well organized and follows a consistent plan. Material is presented in a clear, systematic manner. Four projective uses of the drawings are described. Numerous specimens illustrate the projection of personality, self in relation to others, groups values, and attitudes. A schema for assessment is applied to each drawing; overall impression percedes the identification of specific indicators. The authors recognize the need for integration of the drawing assesment with other methods of evaluation. The importance of the first overall or global impression conveyed by the drawings is duly acknowledged as more meaningful than a specific indicator.

Klepsch and Logie are to be complimented on their carefully researched, well written, comprehensive survey of the field, and on their personal contributions. The procedures for administering the assessments and their underlying rationale are clearly and adequately outlined.

To those beginning a study of the projective uses of child art, this work offers the necessary contextual information. Professionals already actively engaged in interpretation may refer to it for reliable, current information on the state of the art.

Joseph H. Di Leo, M.D.

REFERENCES

Burns, R. C. & Kaufman, S. H. *Kinetic family drawings (K-F-D)*. New York: Brunner/Mazel, 1970.

Burns, R. C. & Kaufman, S. H. *Actions, styles and symbols in kinetic family drawings*. New York: Brunner/Mazel, 1972.

Goodenough, F. L. *Measurement of intelligence by drawings*. New York: World Book Co., 1926.

Harris, D. B. *Children's drawings as measures of intellectual maturity*. New York: Harcourt, Brace & World, 1963.

Harris, D. B. & Roberts, J. *Intellectual maturity of children: Demographic and socio-metric factors* (DHEW, Vital and Health Statistics Series 11, No. 116). Washington, D.C.: U.S. Government Printing Office, 1972.

Katzaroff, M.D. Qu'est-ce que les enfants dessinent? *Arch. de Psychol.* 9:125-233. 1909-1910.

Kerschensteiner, D. G. *Die Entwickelung der zeichnerischen Begabung*. Munich: Gerber, 1905.

Koppitz, E. M. *Psychological evaluation of children's human figure drawings*. New York: Grune & Stratton, 1968.

Levinstein, S. *Kinderzeichnungen bis zum 14 Lebensjahr*. Leipzig: R. Voigtlander Verlag. 1905.

Luguet, G. H. *Les Dessins d'un Enfant: étude psychologique*. Librairie Felix Alcan, Paris, 1913.

Machover, K. *Personality projection in the drawing of the human figure*. Springfield: C. C. Thomas, 1949.

Partridge, L. Children's drawings of men and women. In E. Barnes (Ed.), *Studies in education*. 2:163-179. 1902.

Ricci, C. *L'Arte dei Bambini*. Bologna: Zanichelli editore, 1887.

Sully, J. *Studies of childhood*. London: Longmans, Green, 1895.

CONTENTS

PREFACE

Children Draw and Tell grew out of one author's longstanding fascination with children's drawings and the other author's encouragement of his work in an area which, she believed, was rich in exciting possibilities. Marvin Klepsch, an early childhood psychologist, uses drawings in his clinical practice and finds them a source of considerable information. This book is based partly on his doctoral dissertation dealing with children's human figure drawings (HFDs) and partly on the drawings which he has personally gathered over the years. Laura Logie, a former health educator with a keen interest in psychology, has written many articles on drama, health, and the arts for Saskatchewan newspapers. She felt that most of the HFD information to date has been directed primarily to psychologists trained in projective techniques. Both authors agreed that the time was ripe to make it available in a suitable form to child care professionals who do not have this training but who, glimpsing the potential value of the technique, are eager to learn more about it.

Klepsch has talked on this topic many times to psychologists, teachers, social workers, public health nurses, dentists, dental nurses, preschool teachers, and physicians. All are intrigued by the statements made by drawings. Many had not previously thought of drawings as a source of nonverbal communication or as expressive grapho-motor behavior. Others, although they had made some use of drawings as a measure of personality, were unaware of other projective uses.

Part I of this book deals with the background and theory of projective psychology. Chapter 1 discusses art as a projective technique and emphasizes that all our behavior, including drawings, reflects our personality, attitudes and values. Chapter 2 examines the major ways of getting information about people, and stresses that no one method should be used in isolation; rather, the use of several methods is recommended for best results. Chapter 3 is a brief overview of the major projective and non-projective uses of drawings.

Part II examines in detail the four projective uses of children's drawings. Chapter 4 looks at drawings as a measure of personality. In Chapter 5, group drawings are discussed as a measure of self in relation to others. Chapter 6 is about the use of drawings as a measure of group values, while Chapter 7 deals with drawings as a measure of attitudes. Each of these chapters contains related research, instructions for administration, directions for interpretation, and examples of children's drawings. Chapter 8 ends the book with some concluding thoughts on the projective uses of drawings.

It should be noted that the "child" (or "subject" or "drawer") is referred to as "he" throughout the text, in order to free the writing from unnecessary clutter. Unless a specific sex is being discussed, "he" should be taken to imply "he or she," "his" to imply "his or her," and "himself" to imply "himself or herself."

The chapter on attitudes, based on Klepsch's original study, makes *Children Draw and Tell* unique in that for the first time all *four* projective uses of HFDs are discussed and applied together. The authors hope that the book will be of value to interested readers and prompt them to begin using drawings to help them understand children better.

ACKNOWLEDGEMENTS

The contributions of the following people are gratefully acknowledged:

Dr. E.R. Simpson, a former Director and Medical Health Officer of Saskatchewan Health, Community Health Services, North Battleford Region, for introducing me to Koppitz's book, *Psychological Evaluation of Children's Human Figure Drawiangs*, when I was a fledgling psychologist.

Dr. I.D. Welch, my advisor at the University of Northern Colorado, for making me aware of his own work on drawings and encouraging me to study the subject further.

Drs. E. Copeland, M. Jacobs and *E. Koplitz*, members of my dissertation committee, for their help with the preparation of the dissertation on children's human figure drawings.

Anne Rowley, Public Health Nurse, North Battleford Health Region, for assistance in examining and scoring the drawings of dentists, doctors, and nurses.

M.E.K.

Winifred Webb, a former member of the North Battleford Health Region's office staff, whose friendship and secretarial services we have shared for some years, for the countless hours devoted to typing for us. Since we find each other's handwriting more or less unintelligible, Winifred's unique gift of being able to decipher both manuscripts made her indispensable to the project!

L.D.L.
M.E.K.

CHILDREN DRAW AND TELL

An Introduction to the

Projective Uses of

Children's Human Figure Drawings

PART I

THE THEORY

CHAPTER 1

ART IS PICTORIAL LANGUAGE

Written and spoken languages depend on words to communicate meaning, feelings, and emotions. Other forms of language do not – like the language of mathematics, the language of love, the language of flowers, or body language. For the purposes of this book, language is given its broadest meaning. It is *Every action which proceeds from the human body,* for we communicate not only with words but with unconscious gestures, ways of sitting, standing and walking, styles of dancing and handwriting, choreography, creative writing, music, and art.

Whether the subject wills it or not, the self is projected into each of these activities and revealed to the careful observer. Unconscious gestures, for example, can betray a person's real feelings or state of mind. True, the eyes and face can sometimes deceive or mask what is really being experienced. The rest of the body, however, is usually more truthful. Ekman and Friesen (1969), gestural language scientists, attribute this to the fact that the face receives some basic training in childhood, while the rest of the body does not. To illustrate: If, as a child, you had registered extreme distaste on being instructed to kiss some ugly old lady, you would no doubt have been told in no uncertain terms to straighten up your face. Besides, you may have found it convenient to cultivate a blank or innocent look for purposes of your own. Unlike the face, the rest of the body does not receive the same practice in the art of deception. So while the face may be telling one story, unconscious gestures like the fluttering of the hand, the tapping of a foot, or jerky body movements may be the giving the true account of what is going on inside.

Long before these gestures of deceit were demonstrated experimentally, Sigmund Freud recognized them for what they were. The author of *Language*, David Thomson (1975), quotes him as having once said, "He who has eyes to see and ears to hear may convince himself that no mortal can keep a secret. If his lips are silent, he chatters with his fingertips; betrayal oozes out of him at every pore." In other words, even if there is no speech and the face refuses to tell, the rest of the body can leak information about the person and what may be happening inside the self. In particular, the hand can doodle involuntarily. It can also *draw* voluntarily. The challenge is to learn how to read what is drawn.

A drawing captures symbolically on paper some of the subject's thoughts and feelings. It makes a portion of the inner self visible. The very lines, timidly, firmly, boldly or savagely drawn, give us some information. More is revealed by the content, which is largely determined by the way the subject, consciously or unconsciously, perceives himself and significant other people in his life.

The important point about this self-revelation is that the drawer does not have to be drawing himself. He may be drawing just "a person" or his teacher or his dentist or members of his family. Unwittingly, he sketches in some details of his own traits, attitudes, behavior characteristics, personality strengths and weaknesses. In other words, he leaves an imprint, however incomplete, of his inner self upon his drawing.

This is true of artists far more sophisticated than the young drawers featured in *Children Draw and Tell*. Consider, for example, William Turner, the English painter of so many superb watercolor landscapes. He depicted people (when he used them at all) either drowned or huddled in thunderstorms or as insignificant specks in the picture. It is interesting to note that he was a gnarled gnome of a man with plain features and keen gray eyes. Taciturn, reclusive, and stingy, he was further burdened with an incurably insane mother. On the contemporary scene, no one looking at the works of Allen Sapp, the noted Saskatchewan Cree Indian painter from our own community, would deny that his cold, snowy, desolate landscapes reflect the rigors of his childhood on the reserve, or that his human figures speak of dignity in hardship, and the Indian way of life as it used to be.

To the astute observer, artists speak eloquently of themselves in pictorial language, just as writers speak in word language and composers in the language of musical sounds. In every case, the work reflects the person. Since drawing also reflects the person, the idea of using it as a measurement of personality, of self in relation to others, of group values, and of attitude is not out of line. Its use is all the more valid when one considers that children are able to convey in their drawings thoughts and feelings they cannot possibly express in speech or writing. They simply do not have the words with which to do it, and like our ancient ancestors, must learn to draw before they learn to write. Long before written language existed, man scratched drawings on cave walls to record his feelings, needs, and actions.

Drawing communication, then, is elemental and basic. It is also universal. In modern times, it has had a remarkable growth and can cross any existing language barrier with the greatest of ease. Wherever we travel in the world, signs, symbols and pictures tell us where to phone, camp, eat, drink, sleep, exchange currency, obtain information, where the washrooms and nonsmoking areas are – all without the aid of words.

The topic of a recent Canadian Broadcasting Company *Man Alive* program was the plight of Lebanese children orphaned by war. These children were born in wartime and have lived in a war environment ever since. A wise, compassionate man in charge of one of the many preschool orphanages makes drawing a routine activity for the youngsters. The purpose is not so much to measure as to provide a release for their feelings and hostilities. As one might expect, the drawings feature war planes attacking, bombs exploding, and tanks on the march. The people depicted are all armed with weapons of some sort. One little child draws a white dove pierced through with an arrow, from the tip of which drops of red blood are falling. What more can one say? *Art is pictorial language.*

CHAPTER 2

UNCOVERING INSIDE INFORMATION

MORE THAN ONE WAY

Drawing speaks louder than words in the early stages of a child's development. It is, therefore, ideally suitable as a technique for uncovering information about the inner self. Besides, most children like to draw, which makes the technique an easy one to administer. However, drawing is by no means the only way to gain insight into personality, perception of self in relation to others, group values and attitudes. There are, in fact, three main ways of doing this: *self-report, observation,* and *projective techniques,* of which drawing is but one.

1. Self-report Technique

The child is asked directly about his thought and feelings in as simple a way as possible. The questions are often put verbally in an interview. In the case of an older child, they may be written. The following sample questions (or other items requiring a response) are typical of tests, readily available on the market, which attempt to measure school attitude, personality, or perception of parents:

> *To Measure School Attitude (answer Yes or No)*
> Do you like school?
> Is school fun?
> Does your teacher care about you?
> School is boring.
> Teachers talk too much.

To Measure Personality (answer Yes or No)
    I like to fight.
    I like belonging to lots of different groups.
    People say I'm too loud and noisy.
    I like to play with boys and girls.
    When I am alone and hear a strange noise, I am frightened.

To Measure Perception of Parents
    If you were sick and had to go to a doctor, would you ask
        your mother or father to go with you?
    Whom would you ask to help you with your homework
        – mother or father?
    Who do you think is a happier person, your mother or your
        father?
    If you were unhappy and needed someone to talk to, would
        you go to your mother or your father?

The trouble with self-report is that the implications of the answers may be fairly obvious to the child. As a result, the responses could be consciously controlled. In addition, items of this nature are susceptible to a response set, in which some children will consistently tend to agree or disagree with the items regardless of their content. Sometimes a child may have to choose between more responses than just Yes or No, e.g. Yes, Not Sure, No, or Yes, Usually, Sometimes, No. In such cases, he may tend to select the alternative which appears in a particular position and to give either extreme responses or weak, noncommittal ones.

2. Observation Technique

This differs from the self-report technique in that the child's personality, perceptions, values and attitudes are *inferred* by observation of his behavior. By rating the child in various areas, one is able to get a measurement of what he is like. Rating scales have been devised to measure different aspects of the child's behaviour.

To Measure School Attitude
        (Child is rated on a 5-point scale according to the degree
        of each behaviour)
    Volunteers answers
    Dawdles and procrastinates
    Is discourteous to teachers
    Writes on the desk

9

To Measure Personality (rating is Yes or No)
    Cries easily
    Shy
    Whines and complains
    Shares with other children
    Is aggressive and hits out at others

To Measure Perception of Peers (rating is Yes, Sometimes, No)
    Does child initiate contact with peers?
    Does he get along better with adults than agemates?
    Does he express feelings about others?
    Does he participate in informal, playground games?

Observational techniques are not without certain persistent problems. Some raters tend to err in a particular direction. They may be too severe, too cautious, or too generous. The result is little variation in scores among the children. Again, many tend to be influenced by the overall "quality" of the child. A child who is liked will probably receive high ratings in all areas being assessed. This "halo" effect obscures the strengths and weaknesses of the traits being measured. Finally, ratings are often suspect since raters who know what the ratings are to be used for may be influenced by this knowledge. This is particularly true when children's attitudes are being rated.

3. Projective Technique

These include measures such as sentence completion tests, interpretation of pictures, word association tests, interpretation of play, and drawing techniques. The basic assumptions underlying this approach are that the relatively ambiguous nature of the materials used enables the child to make responses he would otherwise find difficult, and that, in responding, he organizes his material in terms of his own motivations, perceptions, attitudes, and other aspects of his personality. An example of one projective method is showing a child a picture of a family or of a classroom and then asking him to tell a story about the picture. It is assumed that the child projects himself in the story and, in fact, talks about himself, his school, or his family. Questioning the child about the story may bring out additional information.

Some psychologists question the basic assumption that the child's responses, even if spontaneous and undistorted, reflect his own personality, perceptions, values, and attitudes. However, where the projective use of children's drawings is concerned, we are convinced of the value of this technique. Verbal and writing skills are open to deliberate modification by the subject in a way that drawing is not. Moreover, where these skills are lacking or insufficient, drawing offers an important alternative for self-expression. However imperfect, it seems to be able to bring out information about a child which no other technique can.

It has another advantage too. According to a study by Brannigan, Margolis and Moran (1979), drawing is not biased against impulsive children, as some other tests seem to be. When the drawings of impulsive and reflective groups of children were compared (using several variables which indicate impulsiveness), no significant differences were found. This finding convinced these authors that drawings would be useful for general screening.

MULTIPLE APPROACH NEEDED

Since no one technique can adequately assess a child's personality, perceptions, values and attitudes, a multiple-measures approach should always be used. In trying to measure attitude, for example, it would be unwise to rely on drawings alone. Drawings should be supplemented with information from another projective measure, from observation, from an interview or from an objective type of test. Many writers on this topic agree on the need for multiple measures: Ball (1971); Cook and Selltiz (1964); Kahn (1978), Webb, Campbell, Schwartz, and Sechrest (1966). The types of measures used will depend upon the child. For quiet, shy children who do not like to talk, drawings and observational approaches would likely be the best. For those with speech and language difficulties, again the use of drawings and observation would be indicated. Some highly verbal children would likely respond well to interview or direct procedures, as well as to drawings.

THE UNIQUE ROLE OF DRAWINGS

Drawings add a dimension not tapped by self-report or observation techniques, the dimension of fantasy and imagination. While the use of several measures is always recommended, drawing should without fail be one of them. Drawings are easy to obtain, since most children love to draw; they are especially valuable in the case of young children because of their limited language; they dig deeper into whatever aspect is being measured; and they seem to be able to plumb the inner depths of a person and uncover some of the otherwise inaccessible inside information.

11

CHAPTER 3

USES OF HUMAN
FIGURE DRAWINGS

Much may be learned about children's personalities, perceptions, values, and attitudes from *all* of their drawings. However, since we believe that human figure drawings (HFDs) are the richest source of information, we have used them exclusively for the purposes of this book. These drawings may be a person, a particular individual such as a doctor, a dentist, or nurse, or of a group of people, such as family, friends, and classmates.

PROJECTIVE USES

We believe there are four projective uses for children's human figure drawings:

1. *As a Measure of Personality:* By examining the drawing of a person, one can derive information about the uniqueness of the drawer and discover how the drawer sees himself.
2. *As a Measure of Self in Relation to Others:* Group drawings are useful if one wants to find out how a child perceives himself within the particular group drawn. When children draw themselves along with their family or friends or teacher or schoolmates, they project into their drawings their view of themselves in relation to the others in the group.
3. *As a Measure of Group Values:* The drawing of a person also provides clues to group values, since children tend to

draw the kind of individual they most admire or respect. This opens up a whole new area for investigation. One could look at drawings of different cultural and racial groups to find out what kind of people are most often drawn. One could compare the drawings of black children and white children to see if there are distinct differences. Some other interesting questions could be raised: Does each race tend to draw a different kind of man? Is there a universal perception of what a person is like? Does a black child draw people with negroid features or does an Indian child draw an Indian-like person?

4. *As a Measure of Attitudes:* By having children draw specific people with whom they come in contact, one can learn what their attitudes are toward these people. Children's drawings of teachers, doctors, dentists, and nurses, for example, reveal their feelings about these particular professional people.

NONPROJECTIVE USES

HFDs can be used to measure a child's developmental or intellectual maturity. This is the use most familiar to elementary school teachers, public health nurses, and pediatricians. It first attracted attention between 1900 and 1915, a time of increased activity in the child study movement. Two important findings were made during this period: The order of development in the drawings of children is constant; and children of lower ability generally make inferior drawings.

Goodenough (1926) published the first test for systematically evaluating children's drawings on a point scale method. Harris (1963) revised and extended this procedure, which became known as the Goodenough-Harris Draw-a-Man Test. Using this test, various researchers have found that, as children increase in age, so does the detail in their drawings. The legs, arms, head, and trunk are also drawn more in proportion. Scoring systems for estimating IQ from figure drawings have been developed by Buck (1948) for the House-Tree-Person Test and by Koppitz (1968) for HFDs by children ages five to 11. As a matter of fact, it is interesting to note that Dunleavy, Hanson, and Szasz (1981) found Koppitz's scoring system useful for identifying kindergarten children who were not ready for school.

One of the tools considered most valuable in assessing school readiness is the Gesell Incomplete Man Test. It is part of the Gesell developmental and behavioral evaluation as described by Ilg and Ames (1978). The drawing of a man is also part of the Denver Developmental Screening Test, a widely used screening instrument

13

devised by Frankenburg and Dodds (1975) to detect developmental disorders in children from birth through five years of age.

The scoring systems in all these measures are based on the assumption that, as individuals grow older and mature, their drawings reflect the developmental changes. School and environment are said to have little effect on the drawings and artistic ability. Harris views the HFD as a measure of intellectual or conceptual maturity. He describes this maturity as the ability to perceive or discriminate similarities and differences, to abstract or classify objects according to similarities and differences, and to generalize or assign a discriminated object to a correct class.

Drawing Ages and Stages

The first attempts to draw the human figure are simplified and incomplete representations. A three-year-old typically draws a person as a head, the reason being that, at this age, the head is the most important to the child. Often eyes, a nose, and mouth are drawn on the face. Four-year-olds make tadpole-like drawings, and appendages representing arms and legs are added to the drawing of a head. Gardner (1980) describes tadpole figures as having two protuberances at the bottom representing legs and two extensions on the side which may be seen as arms, but suggest that the central circle may stand for either a head or a body. At five years of age, most children will draw a body and a head. The head will contain eyes, a nose, and a mouth, and arms and legs will emanate from the body.

At each successive age, additional features, such as neck, fingers, ears, pupils, etc., will be added on. One-dimensional features will become two-dimensional. Proportion among various body parts will change. For example, while five-year-olds will usually draw a large head, more mature children will draw the head in proportion with the rest of the body. Greater pencil control develops with age and this is reflected in better line quality, i.e., firmness, sureness, quality of line juncture.

In most scoring systems, a point is given for each developmental indicator present. The totaled score indicates a child's status relative to others.

Strangely enough, according to Leichtman (1979), adults are unable to draw like children aged three through five; however, according to Arkell (1976b), they are able to draw like children aged five through ten!

PART II

THE APPLICATION

CHAPTER 4

DRAWINGS AS A
MEASURE OF
PERSONALITY

RESEARCH TO DATE

Introducing the Draw-a-Person Test (DAP)

Karen Machover (1949) was the first to analyze human figure draw-ings (HFDs) with a view to measuring the projected self. Her analyses were based on the body-image hypothesis. She believed the human figure drawn by the individual directed to "draw a person" related in-timately to the impulses, anxieties, conflicts, and compensations char-acteristic of that individual. In a way, the figure drawn *is* the person, and the paper, the environment.

According to this hypothesis, various sensations, perceptions, and emotions are located in certain body parts. As a result, the body-image is developed. Prytula, Phelps, Morrissey and Davis (1978) say this im-age, since it is formed out of the individual's unique experiences, guides the drawer, providing a natural vehicle for the expression of body needs and conflicts.

Machover paid particular attention to certain aspects of a drawing, such as: size of figure; placement on the page; rapidity of graphic movement; pencil pressure; solidarity and variability of lines used; the succession of parts drawn; the use of background; spontaneity or rigidity; whether the figure was drawn in profile or frontal view. In analysis, she considered the properties of each part of the body, the tendency toward incompletions, the amount of placement of detail, the amount and focus of line reinforcements, erasures and line changes, the degree of symmetry, the treatment of the midline, the mood expressed in the face or posture of the figure. Certain meanings became attached to specific body parts. The head, for example, was considered the location of the self and the center of intellectual power, social dominance, and control of body impulses. Large heads might be drawn by those suffering from organic brain damage or by those placing great importance on intellectual achievement.

In a later work, Machover (1953) focused on the drawings of children and traced their development with children aged five through 11. The drawings of public school middle-class children, public school black children and Jewish private school children were compared.

Scoring and Interpreting the DAP Test

The body-image hypothesis gave rise to a number of scoring and interpretative systems. Urban (1963) produced a catalogue for the interpretation of the Draw-a-Person (DAP) Test, deriving much of his material from Bender, Buck, Goodenough, Hammer and Machover. A similar catalogue was devised by Jolles (1971) for the House-Tree-Person (HTP) Test. While his interpretations are presented somewhat dogmatically, Jolles does point out that many of them are only hypotheses and must be used in the context of all other factors of the HTP Test, together with a case history and complete background of the individual.

More recently, a handbook was written by Ogden (1975) to assist practitioners in evaluating personality. The section on projective drawings was well researched. Ogden stressed that his book should be used only by persons with a thorough grounding in clinical and projective psychology. As to the use of a specific indicator, he warned against doing this in isolation and out of context.

Some researchers have focused on the HFDs of special children. Basing their interpretations on the findings of Machover and Koppitz, authors Schildkrout, Shenker and Sonnenblick (1972) examined specifically the personality traits of disturbed youngsters, aged 12 to 18. The problems they studied were those of sexual identity, physical illness, organicity, neurosis, psychosis, and depression as manifested in the adolescents' drawings. Di Leo (1973), on the other hand, uses the drawings of the learning-disabled, dyslexic, mentally retarded, neurologically impaired, sensory-impaired and physically disabled to gain a deeper insight into these children's special concerns and to diagnose deviations from normality.

Actually, it was Koppitz (1966a, 1968) who developed the first

18

refined scoring system for evaluating the drawings of young children. In differentiating children with emotional problems from normals, she considered 30 emotional indicators significant. In a validity study, she found that the emotional indicators occurred more often in the drawings of children attending a guidance clinic than in the drawings of well-adjusted students. The presence of two or more of these indicators was found to be highly suggestive of emotional problems and unsatisfactory interpersonal relationships.

The Koppitz system scores three types of items:

1. items that relate to the quality of the drawing, such as the type of line, integration, shading, asymmetry of lines, size of figures, slant of figure and transparencies;
2. items or features not usually found on HFDs, including tiny or large heads, crossed eyes, teeth, short or long arms, big hands, clinging arms, legs pressed together, genitals, monster-like figures and clouds, snow or rain;
3. omissions of items, such as eyes, nose, mouth, body, arms, legs and neck.

Pate and Nichols (1971) developed a scoring sheet to help those already familiar with the Koppitz scoring procedures. In 1970, Engle and Suppes developed a *weighted* scoring system. Indicators, instead of just being scored as present or absent, were weighted according to their previously demonstrated predictive power. In all, they identified 27 items as anxiety indicators. The total HFD score was correlated with the Test Anxiety Scale for Children, a self-report measure of anxiety. A low but significant relationship was found. When this system was used in a study of children's responses to dental treatment, Sonnenberg and Venham (1977) also found a low but significant correlation between the HFD score and the score on a self-report measure. The HFD score also related significantly to heart rate, basal skin response, and clinical ratings of anxiety.

The Evanston Early Identification Scale (EEIS) was devised by Dillard and Landsman (1968) to predict school problems from the HFDs of kindergarten children. Through this early screening device, the authors hoped to identify pupils who should be referred for special help because of academic, perceptual, or emotional difficulties. The 10 items (scored if missing) and their respective weights were: Hair (1), eyes (2), nose (2), mouth (3), arms (2), hands (2), legs (1), feet (2), body (4), correct position of body parts (2). When the respective mean EEIS scores of those referred and those not referred were compared, the referred children had significantly higher means. Since there were no significant differences between the mean IQs of the two groups, the results were not influenced by intelligence.

Apfeldorf, Walter, Kaimen, Smith and Arnett (1974) devised a method of evaluating affective responses to HFDs. In contrast to other systems, this method took into account the number of affective responses present when a rater was first presented with a drawing. According to the authors, while two drawings may contain the same formal scoreable content, they may elicit different impressions and evaluations from the rater. The need for training prospective raters was discussed.

Sexual Identification on the DAP

It is generally believed that an HFD is an expression of self- or body-image. When asked to draw a person, children usually draw their own self sex. They also draw those to whom they feel close, as is the case with very young children who often draw their mother. Machover (1949) believed that if a child drew a figure of a different sex than his own, he could be experiencing difficulties with normal sexual identification.

Schildkrout et al. (1972) maintained that girls have less sense of sexual identity than boys. They suggested that adolescent girls go through a period of bisexuality when they are less defended than boys in regard to this sexual confusion. Phelan (1964) claimed that sixth grade boys who drew the opposite sex were from homes with a weak father, were dependent and viewed themselves as being dominated, felt inadequate, had a poor attitude toward their father, and/or were from homes with dominating mothers.

Research studies consistently tell us that the majority of boys and girls draw their own sex when asked to draw a person. Heinrich and Triebe (1972) found this to be true in every one of the 19 studies they reviewed. They also found sex differences beginning at around age 11, with adolescent boys more frequently drawing same-sex figures than adolescent girls. Bieliauskas (1960) examined 1000 HFDs from children aged four through 14 years. He, too, found that both sexes favored their own sex when drawing a person. The tendency to do this increased with age, particularly after age nine, although the developmental pattern was more stable for boys than girls. An earlier study by Weider and Nolles (1953) had resulted in the same finding. However, in this case, there were differences between the boys and the girls: 70 percent of the boys drew their own sex first, while 94 percent of the girls drew their self-sex first. The differences were statistically significant. Tolor and Tolor (1974) gave the Draw-a-Person task

20

to 232 public school children. The results indicated that 91 percent of the boys drew their own sex, while 94 percent of the females drew their own sex. The authors attributed the large number of girls drawing their own sex to the Women's Liberation Movement! Brown (1979), in a study using 366 children ages five through 11, found that girls drew female figures 88 percent of the time, while boys drew male figures 94 percent of the time. Younger boys drew more females, perhaps because of greater involvement with the mother. Girls ages nine and 10 drew more males. The authors speculated that the reason might be either more involvement with their fathers or an attempt to compete with their brothers for their father's affection. Fisher (1961) found that delinquent adolescent boys, who drew female figures first when asked to "draw a person and then a person of the opposite sex," had a significantly greater incidence of nudity in both figures.

Sexual ambiguity in HFDs was the concern of Rierdan and Koff (1981). When 461 children in grades five through nine were asked to draw a person and indicate the sex of the person, eight percent of them were unable to classify their drawings as to sex. The researchers attitbuted this to an ill-defined sexual identity. In their opinion, the children who express uncertainty about their drawings require further investigation.

Hammer and Kaplan (1964a) were particularly interested in examining the reliability of the sex drawn. They found that children who draw an opposite-sex figure one time do not necessarily do this the next time. Litt and Margoshes (1966) replicated this study, except that the children were asked to draw on three different occasions instead of only two. Like Hammer and Kaplan, they found considerable variability in their drawings and urged caution in interpreting opposite-sex drawings as a measure of sexual identification.

Validity of the DAP

For Scoring Systems

The validity of the Koppitz scoring system has been tested by several investigators. Snyder and Gaston (1970) advised caution in its use, particularly in drawing inferences about personality from specific indicators. They reported finding elevated and rigid figures (both considered by Koppitz as indicators of anxiety) in 31 to 62 percent of the 680 drawings of the entire first-grade population from nine schools. Pihl and Nimrod (1976) found relatively high correlations between raters using the Koppitz system but questioned the validity of the procedure. No relationship was found between the score on a drawing

21

and all but one subtest score of the Children's Personality Questionnaire (Porter and Cattell, 1963). The exception was the anxiety score, which had a low correlation. Hall and Ladriere (1970) compared six different systems for scoring young children and found that only the Koppitz and Evanston Early Identification Scale (EEIS) systems significantly distinguished between problem and non-problem children. The authors said that the choice between the two must be based on considerations such as normative developmental orientation, which is the strength of the Koppitz system, or scoring ease and brevity, which are the advantages of the EEIS.

The validity of the Machover DAP technique was studied by Blum (1954). The DAP score was compared with ratings by psychiatrists, a battery of psychological tests, and rating scales. The DAP was found to have questionable validity but proved no worse than the other common clinical assessment procedures used.

For Shy and Aggressive Children: According to Koppitz (1966b), nine HFD indicators significantly differentiated shy and aggressive children. These were gross asymmetry of limbs, the presence of teeth, long arms, big hands, genitals, tiny figure, hands cut off, and the omission of the nose and mouth. The first five appeared only in the drawings of aggressive subjects. A similar study by Lingren (1971) did not replicate these results, perhaps due to sampling differences. The Koppitz sample was drawn from children in a Mental Health Clinic, while Lingren used a sample of non-clinic children.

For Predicting Acting-out Behavior: Hammer (1980), from his years of clinical experience and research, finds drawing useful in predicting "acting-out" behavior. He regards other projective tests such as the Thematic Apperception Test (TAT) or the Rorschach as inadequate for this purpose. The information gained from the stories told in response to the TAT pictures is often about what the subject dreams of doing but never actually does. The Rorschach, while useful for describing what a person is like, is not useful for predicting what a person will do in the future. Only drawings, Hammer maintains, will give us clues to what a person will do at a later date. Drawings are a means of psychomotor release and what is drawn on the page is likely to result in action later on. Indicators viewed as clues to later "acting out" behavior are: *size* – when a drawing is pressing out against the sides of the page, the drawer has difficulty with limits: *sequence* – when drawings start out controlled but end up uncontrolled; *pressure* – heavy pressure; *strokes* – short, aggressive strokes; *symmetry* – a lack of symmetry; *dissociation* – when, for example, a child draws an aggressive person and his verbal description of the drawing shows that he is quite unaware of this.

For Black vs. White Personality Adjustment: Hammer (1953) compared the House-Tree-Person (HTP) drawings of black and white normal children in grades one through eight. He found black children more maladjusted, hostile and aggressive than white. A significantly higher percentage of drawings by black children were space constricted, too large for the page, without adequate space framing them, and touching or almost touching the edge of the page. McHugh (1963) studied the drawings of black, Puerto Rican, and white children. While she found that Puerto Ricans drew smaller persons than whites, she found no indications of frustration and aggression. The evidence for the greater space constriction in blacks' drawings was minimal. McHugh concluded that blacks were not more frustrated and aggressive than whites. A replication of Hammer's study was carried out by Kuhlman and Bieliauskas (1976), who, however, matched their groups for intelligence and socioeconomic status. No significant differences were found between black and white groups' HTP IQ measures or on personality adjustment ratings.

For Organicity: Back in 1956, Reznikoff and Tomblen investigated the degree to which 15 indicators suggestive of organicity characterized the drawings of patients with organic problems, in comparison with drawings of those with psychiatric problems. Five indicators turned up more often among the "organic" group: weak synthesis; parts misplaced; shrunken arms and legs; parts other than the head and extremities distorted; and petal or scribbled fingers. The authors, however, cautioned against relying solely on a sign approach when analyzing drawings.

For Socioeconomic Differences: Using her scoring system, Koppitz (1969) tried to find out if differences in socioeconomic background were related to specific emotional indicators on HFDs. She found that the usual characteristic differences between boys and girls were greater than the differences due to socioeconomic status. It is interesting to note that, in 1980, Szasz, Baade, and Paskewicz found that socioeconomic status was a better predictor of success in kindergarten than either the Koppitz emotional or developmental scores. While cautioning against the exclusive use of drawings in screening for school readiness, they do suggest their use with some populations.

For Anxiety: Several studies have examined the validity of certain specific indicators used to determine the presence of anxiety. Johnson

(1971b) explored the validity of upper lefthand paper placement as an indicator of anxiety. The subjects were administered the Draw-a-Person (DAP) Test and the Institute for Personality and Ability Testing (IPAT) Anxiety Scale. Upper lefthand placement was found significantly more often in those with higher anxiety scores on the IPAT. Opposite results were obtained in a study by Swartz, Laosa and McGavern (1976), who found no relationship between Sarason's Test Anxiety Scale for Children (Sarason et al., 1960) for children and upper leftland drawing placement. Other variables, such as conceptual maturity, cognitive inhibition, and the ability to estimate time, were considered to be related to spatial placement.

The HFDs of "high" and "low" anxious children were studied by Fox, Davidson, Lighthall, Waite, and Sarason (1958). The drawings of the high anxious subjects showed more mutilation and rigidity, and those of low anxious subjects more playfulness, humor, smiling, and arms in down position. While high anxious boys had more shading than low anxious boys, low anxious girls had more shading than the girls who were high in anxiety!

In another study, by Prytula and Hiland (1975), Sarason's General Anxiety Scale for children correlated with specific indicators on the DAP. No significant relationships were found between these measures. The study offered no support for maintaining that head-body ratio, erasures, omissions, and transparencies accurately differentiated normal elementary school children on the basis of general anxiety.

HFDs have been used by Sonnenberg and Venham (1977) to measure children's response to dental treatment. The response to each dental visit was assessed using the HFD as well as five additional measures: heart rate, basal skin response, picture test of anxiety, clinical ratings of anxiety, and a clinical rating of cooperative behavior. The HFD score was significantly related to all the other measures except the cooperative behavior ratings. An interesting finding was that children suppress signs of overt fear and anxiety with increasing age, and this gives a misleading impression of older children's feelings toward their dental experience.

Using the IPAT Anxiety Scale, Johnson (1971a) investigated the validity of three indicators – shading, erasures, and line reinforcement. A significant relationship was found between shading and the IPAT score, but nonsignificant relationships were found for erasures and line reinforcement.

Handler and Reyher (1965) reviewed 51 studies of HFDs with reference to 21 anxiety indicators. The research results seemed to uphold the validity of a number of them – specifically, omission, distortion, detail loss, line presure increase, heavy line, size increase and decrease, head simplification, and trunk simplification. Evidence was less consistent for reinforcement, line discontinuity, light line, vertical imbalance, line absence, and transparency. Some of the studies reviewed recorded significantly less shading, erasure, reinforcement, placement in the upper lefthand corner, and emphasis than had been expected.

In a study of the drawings of both children and their parents, Sopchak (1970) found little relationship between the scores of the two groups. Since differences in development could explain differences between age groups, Saarni and Azara (1977) compared the anxiety indicators found in the drawings of adolescents, young adults, and middle-aged adults. They discovered that the adolescents were much more likely to present more anxiety indicators than the adult groups. There was no difference in this regard between young and middle-aged adults.

For Stress: Handler and Reyher (1964) examined the effect of stress on the drawings of 57 college students. The subjects made drawings of a male, female, and automobile under both stress and non-stress conditions. More anxiety indicators were present in the drawings done under stress than in the non-stress situation. The two drawing patterns that emerged under the stress conditions were constriction and expansion. If anxiety indicators were present in both figures and the automobile, the authors speculated that the anxiety was probably due to external stress. If anxiety indicators were present in the human figure drawings but not in the automobile, the source of anxiety was due to internal stress (subjects use erasure, reinforcement, etc., *to cope* with, rather than avoid, threatening material). If anxiety indicators were present in the automobile but not the figures, the source of anxiety was due to internal stress but the defensive style was *avoidant* rather than coping. The study also found significantly more anxiety when drawing a person than the car.

In another study of the effects of stress on drawings, Sturner and Rothbaum (1980) took as their subjects 68 children, ages four to 12, who were hospitalized for elective surgery. The group of children prepared in advance for stress (in this case a blood test) were able to cope better and had significantly fewer emotional indicators in their drawings than the group who were unprepared for the blood test.

On the subject of stress, Koppitz (1960) had something to say too. She found that the HFD of first-graders whose teacher was tense, unsmiling, and rigid contained more emotional indicators than the drawings of children who had a warm, loving, friendly teacher. We suggest a more direct way to assess the children's attitude toward their teacher would have been to ask them to draw their teacher.

For Self-Esteem: Do human figure drawings actually express self-esteem, and if so, in what way? Coopersmith, Sakai, Beardslee, and Coopersmith (1976) set themselves the task of finding out. On the basis of the Coopersmith Self-Esteem Inventory and a teacher behavior rating scale, they identified five types of self-esteem groups. The HFDs were scored on 15 variables describing their different aspects. There were five significant differences between the higher and lower self-esteem groups. The drawings of those higher in self-esteem contained well-drawn hands, indicated affect, and appropriate social role. They gave an overall impression that they were free from pathology and drawn by a likeable person. It was found, too, that the subjects' behavioral expressions of self-esteem more closely matched the HFD characteristics than did their subjective evaluations. The authors concluded that, while HFDs are indeed associated with self-esteem, the association is not as clear-cut as generally believed.

There have been several studies investigating the relationship between *size* of drawing and self-esteem. Machover claimed that children with high self-esteem drew larger figures than those with low self-esteem. However, Dalby and Vale (1977) found no significant relationship between fifth grade children's scores on the Coopersmith Self-Esteem Inventory and the height of the HFDs. They also found no relationship between the teacher's ratings of self-esteem and the height of the HFDs. They then compared the subject's drawing of himself with the drawings of two friends of the same age. The relative size of the figures appeared unrelated to self-esteem.

Prytula and Thompson (1973) also found no relationship between size of figure and the score on the Coopersmith Self-Esteem Inventory. In their study, children ages 10 through 13 were asked to draw self, man, woman, and Eskimo. They tended to draw the Eskimo larger than the other figures, perhaps (the authors thought) due to the fact that they were unfamiliar with the Eskimo figure. In 1978, Prytula et al. confirmed the previous findings. The variables of size used in the study were body height and width, head size, and total area. Self-concept was measured by the Piers-Harris Scale and the Coopersmith Self-Esteem Inventory.

In his studies, Black (1972) found that the HFD height definitely correlated with chronological age, with actual height, and with perceived height of the subject. He concluded that, while psychodynamic factors may have some influence, age, height, and perceived height were more significantly related to HFD size. Wilee and Davis

26

(1976) took the discussion in a different direction. They pointed out that the size of the HFD could be a function of group versus individual administration! When tested individually, subjects high in self-esteem drew taller and larger figures than those low in self-esteem. When tested in a group, however, there were no differences in size between the HFDs of the two types of subjects.

For Learning-disabled: The drawings of learning-disabled children attracted the special attention of Bachara, Zaba, and Raskin (1975), who found that they contained more emotional indicators than a control group with no learning problems. The learning-disabled group paid more attention to the eyes. Since many of them were perceptually impaired, this suggested a possible awareness of their particular problem.

Wagner (1980), who also studied the HFDs of learning-disabled children, found in them signs of a poor self-image. He divided the drawings into four descriptive categories: Catgory I, "Developmental Immaturity," drawings are typical of those done by younger children. Category II, "Aggression/Withdrawal Tendencies," drawings may be either tiny, insignificant figures or boisterous, ebullient ones. Category III, "Organicity," drawings are sketchy, with empty spaces filled in with shading. Category IV, "Grotesqueness or Bizarreness," drawings contain disproportionate body size, eccentric accessories, or magnified detail.

The *reading*-disabled were the subjects of a special investigation by Stavrianos (1970). Using the House-Tree-Person (HTP) Test, this researcher compared good readers, deficit readers with emotional problems, deficit readers with neurological problems, and deficit readers without neurological problems. Compared with the good readers, the groups with reading problems exhibited fewer normal and more withdrawn, constricted, dependent, and organic patterns. Among the problem readers, the greatest differences were found in the younger boys of average intelligence without neurological impairment! Stavrianos concluded that projective test data can help in the differential diagnosis of reading deficit.

For Deaf and Hearing-impaired: A study comparing the HTP drawings of young deaf and hearing-impaired children was done by Davis and Hoopes (1975). Since the ears and mouth are the special trouble sites for deaf children, the authors expected to see some differences in their representations of these particular features. There were none. Davis and Hoopes suggested that future research of the HTP Test should be directed to the qualitative aspects of the drawings rather than to the development of a checklist of single indicators.

For Obese Subjects: In the case of obese children, Nathan (1973) found that the subjects' drawings of male and female figures were no larger than those of their matched controls. However, qualitative analysis revealed that the drawings of obese children were more undifferentiated and contained more stick figures and a large number of bizarre, distorted representations.

For Physically Handicapped: The studies which follow are based on the assumption that a child will represent his physical self in his drawings, and if he has some kind of physical handicap, he will indicate that in some way.

Wysocki and Whitney (1965) confirmed this assumption and found that crippled children indicated their deformity in some manner. They also found that crippled children expressed more aggression in their drawings but that the intensity of aggression depended on the specific nature of their handicap. Centers and Centers (1963) also found that the majority of limbless children represented themselves realistically and either left out a limb or included a prosthetic device. While their body images differed from those of normal children, their drawings did not contain more indicators of conflict or anxiety. Silverstein and Robinson (1956) used three different methods to determine whether drawings reflected the physical disability of subjects. According to their own examination of the drawings, more than three-quarters of the children represented their disability. However, a comparison of the drawings of the handicapped with those of normals, using 55 indicators, showed a nonsignificant number of differences. Also, experienced judges were unable to differentiate the drawings of disabled and normal children. Johnson and Wawrzaszek (1961) found that drawings which received higher IQ ratings (greater detail and perspective) were often considered as normal, when comparing drawings of the physically handicapped with normals. The drawings of handicapped children tended to be somewhat larger.

In order to find out if the drawings of poliomyelitis patients reflected their disability, Johnson and Greenberg (1978) gave the Draw-a-Man Test to polio patients and their matched controls. No significant differences were found between the two groups when the drawings were rated for quality. Of the 17 variables rated in an analysis of variance, only one was significant for the disability group. The authors concluded that quality may sometimes mask the projective aspect in HFDs.

The verbal descriptions of handicapped and normal children's drawings of a house, tree and person were compared by Wawrzaszek, Johnson, and Sciera (1958). They found no differences between the two groups.

For Congenital Heart Disease Children: The size of the drawings of children with cardiac disease was compared with the size of drawings of normal, retarded and emotionally disturbed children. Children with heart disease typically depicted themselves smaller than the normal children. This finding led authors Green and Levitt (1962) to infer that children with heart disease have a constricted view of their bodies.

For Encephalitic Children: Bender (1940) found the drawings of non-retarded children with encephalitis similar to those done by the mentally retarded. The drawings were lacking in detail and showed poor eye-hand skills.

For Mentally Retarded: The body image of normal and retarded children was investigated by Wysocki and Wysocki (1973). The children ranged in age from nine to 13 years. Mean IQ for the retarded group was 61 and for the normal group 102. The drawings of the retarded group were larger in size; contained fewer erasures, less clothing, less detail; were less symmetrical; demonstrated a rigid, horizontal positioning of arms. Normal children's drawings were smaller in size; contained more erasures, more clothing and more detail; were more symmetrical; and the arm position was more fluid. Bellamy and Daly (1969) also found a relationship between size of figure and IQ. With an increase in IQ, there was a corresponding decrease in the size of the HFD. Ottenbacher (1981) found that the size of the figure drawn was related to self-concept. Females tended to have better self-concepts than males, and the size of the figure, as well as the overall DAP score, was related to self-concept as measured by the Piers-Harris Self-Concept Scale. Subjects with poorer self-concepts tended to produce smaller drawings. Finally, De Martino (1954), in comparing the drawings of retarded, homosexual males with those of retarded, heterosexual males, found more eyelashes and high heels in the homosexuals' drawings.

For Emotionally Handicapped: Koppitz demonstrated the validity of 30 drawing indicators in differentiating emotionally handicapped clinic patients from well-adjusted school children. A cross-validation study of Fuller, Preuss and Hawkins (1970) supported her contention that emotional indicators occur more often in the drawings of disturbed children, but did not support the view that two or more indicators suggested emotional problems and poor interpersonal relationships. Fifty-eight percent of the emotionally disturbed group either had one indicator or none in their drawings. They would have qualified as normal if two or more indicators had been the cut-off point.

Springer (1941), using the Goodenough scale, was unable to differntiate between the drawings of the adjusted and the maladjusted. He did, however, find a tendency for the maladjusted to include more detail in their drawings, while the adjusted were slightly better on items involving motor coordination and correct proportions. The drawings of different kinds of emotionally disturbed children were compared by McHugh (1966). Neurotics drew small, slight figures and placed them farther from the bottom of the page that did the children with conduct disturbances. While all of the conduct disturbance children drew their self-sex, neurotic boys often drew female figures.

Machover suggested that eye-ear emphasis on the DAP was suggestive of paranoia. However paranoid hospitalized patients did not emphasize these parts in their drawings, so the validity of this indicator was seriously questioned by Griffith and Peyman (1959) and Ribler (1957).

Reliability of the DAP

Many of the HFD scoring systems can be used reliably with high interrater reliability. In the Klepsch (1979) study, 264 drawings were scored independently by two raters. Each drawing was scored for 13 indicators and the percentage of agreement between the two raters was 91 percent.

Hammer and Kaplan (1966) were interested in another aspect of reliability. They had over 1300 children in grades four, five, and six draw a person and then a person of the opposite sex. One week later, they had the children repeat this task. The investigators wanted to find out if the children drew the figures the same both times. The following indicators were found to be reliable, i.e., the same on both administrations: missing fingers; heads without bodies; upper, lower and left placement on a page; shading; erasures; type of mouth; frontal view drawings. Indicators found unreliable or different on each administration were: the omission of hands, feet and nose; placement on the right side of the page; the drawing of teeth; right profile drawings. With regard to sex differences, boys exceeded girls in shading, drawing heads without bodies, drawing teeth, and right-facing profile drawings. Girls exceeded boys in leaving out body parts and had a tendency to erase more.

Effect of Training

Effect of Perceptual Training: Some researchers have examined the influence of perceptual training on children's drawing scores. Coyle, Clance, and Joesting (1977) found that perceptual enrichment activities did not significantly increase scores on the Goodenough-Harris Draw-a-Man Test. The activities consisted of body awareness exercises, imaging of body parts, and air tracing of these parts. Miller, Sabatino, and Miller (1977) also found that special training in visual perception did not influence scores. The 14 visual-perceptually impaired children who received 30 minutes of daily instruction for a 12-week period received no better scores than their matched controls. Bachara and Zaba (1976) reported that four to six months of training *did*, in fact, influence drawing scores. While pretest results indicated that 35 children had more Koppitz emotional indicators than their controls, the posttest emotional indicators were similar for both groups.

Effect of Art Factors: Solar, Bruehl, and Kovacs (1970) found a significant correlation between artistic ability as rated by artists on a nine-point scale and the score on the DAP Test. Using fifth grade students, Burns and Velicer (1977) found that art instruction *increased* Goodenough-Harris drawing test scores. The drawing test was administered once before art instruction began and twice after instruction was completed. While no differences were found in the controls between pretest and both posttests, the treatment group showed significant gains on both posttests, as well as a significant *decline* from the first posttest to the second. There was some question as to how long the results would hold up. Bieliauskas and Bristow (1959) found that art training did influence drawing scores. Two groups of college students, one with two or more years of art training and one with no training, were given the HTP test, and the IQs derived from the drawings were scored. While the groups were matched for age, sex and intelligence, the group with art training obtained significantly higher IQ scores. Both Whitmyre (1953) and Sherman (1958) found that the ability to draw influences psychologists' ratings of adjustment. The drawings of normal and psychiatric adult groups were intermingled and psychologists were asked to pick out those made by normal and abnormal individuals. The drawings were also rated for art quality by artists. Figures rated poor in art quality tended to be chosen as abnormal in psychological adjustment, while drawings rated good in art were considered normal in adjustment.

Trained vs. Untrained Interpreters: Several researchers have been interested in comparing the respective abilities of trained and untrained persons to interpret human figure drawings. Arkell (1976a) found no significant differences among teachers, secretaries, seventh grade students, school administrators, and psychologists in differentiating the drawings of maladjusted children from the normal. Striker (1967) found university students more effective than experienced psychologists in correctly classifying the drawings of normal and psychiatric patients! Hiler and Nesvig (1965) found no differences between psychologists and non-psychologists in discriminating the drawings made by a normal and a psychiatric group of adolescents. Psychologists tended to overestimate pathology since they used so many invalid criteria. The authors concluded that more research must be conducted into these criteria. Tolor (1955) found that psychologists were successful at judging popularity from HFDs. Teachers, as a group, were far less successful at this than psychologists, although some individual teachers attained surprisingly good levels of differentiation.

In a study designed to assess the validity of the DAP in differentiating between children with good or poor social adjustments, Ziv and Shechori (1970) found that psychologists did no better than non-psychologists. Psychologists based their judgment on criteria such as proportion, the placement of figure on the page, rigidity, and size, while non-psychologists simply described drawings as neat or nice or correct. Cressen (1975) found no differences between clinical psychologists and college students in correctly classifying the drawings of schizophrenics and normals, and he seriously questioned the validity of the technique.

Highly Trained Interpreters: The validity of clinical judgments based on HFDs was also studied by Wanderer (1969). With the assistance of Machover, Wanderer designated 20 of the highest ranking experts in the U.S.A. as judges. Each judge was asked to choose from among five pairs of drawings – those done by a psychotic, a neurotic, a mental defective, a homosexual and a normal – and to rank each drawing from one to five in the group to which they thought it belonged. The experts were able to identify the mental defectives with an accuracy which ruled out chance, but could not identify the other four groups, even when given a second chance to make a correct diagnosis. The expertness of the judges, as determined from the ranks they were accorded by their peers, was unrelated to their actual performance. Hammer (1969a) criticized the concept behind the Wanderer study and the methods it used. He said that neither Machover nor anyone else had ever intended the DAP to be anything more than a supplement to the verbal techniques.

Since the expert judges in Wanderer's (1969) study were able to pick out the drawings of mental defectives, Adler (1970) studied the cognitive component in HFDs. In a factor analytic study, Adler found that the figure drawing procedure is essentially a test of the cognitive factor only. He therefore concluded that drawing tests should be used to evaluate cognitive maturity, not personality development.

Morris (1955) assessed a group of normal 13-year-old children using the DAP and then assessed them five years later when they were 18 years old. Here are some of his findings: Children at both ages consistently drew their own sex; boys at all ages produced more profile drawings; both boys and girls spent less time on their drawings at age 18; there was a decline in the use of bright colors with increasing age; more girls at both ages tended to omit and hide essential parts of the figures; the body parts most often selected for special treatment were the arms and hands; at 18, boys demonstrated an interest in secondary sexual characteristics, while girls did not.

The age children assigned to their drawings was of particular interest to McHugh (1965). Six hundred normal children ages seven through 11 were asked to draw a person, a person of the opposite sex, and then to indicate the sex and age of each figure. Ages assigned by girls to both sex figures increased progressively with age, while those assigned by boys increased but not progressively. There was a consistent relationship between age assigned to the drawings and the child's own age.

Hammer and Kaplan (1964b) were interested in whether children in grades four, five, and six draw profile or front facing drawings. Girls drew more front views than boys and boys drew more right facing profiles. There were no differences among the drawings of children in the various grades.

Zuk (1962) found that the height and width of drawings increased with age. When examining the drawings of 89 males with a mental age of six through 14, he found the height of figures doubled from mental age six to 14, while the width increased about 50 percent.

A longitudinal study of the development of the body concept was undertaken by Faterson and Witkin (1970). The HFDs of two groups of males and females were examined at ages eight and 13 in one group and at ages 10, 14, 17, and 24 in another. The drawings were rated on the Articulation-of-Body-Concept (ABC) scale, a nine-point scale in which higher ratings are assigned to the more articulated drawings. ABC scores increased between ages eight and 14, with little change thereafter. At the same time, there was marked individual stability in ABC scores, even over a 14-year span. The authors found these results to run parallel to the findings on the development of differentiation in the areas of perception and defenses.

Suns are frequently found on HFDs. They are often thought to represent dependency feelings in the person who draws it. Loney (1971), in examining the drawings of first-graders and sixth-graders, found more suns in the drawings of girls and younger children.

There have been several extensive reviews of literature on the figure drawing technique. Swenson's reviews (1957, 1968) have been unusually thorough and comprehensive. They have dealt with reliability; the validity of the body image hypothesis; methods of evaluating drawings; structural and formal aspects of drawings; and the significance of content in drawings. His earlier review (1957) cast considerable doubt on the value of drawings for personalilty assessment and diagnostic purposes, since little research supported the underlying basic theory, i.e., Machover's body-image hypothesis. However, Swenson's later review, in 1968, which covered the literature between 1957-1966, was more positive. He concluded that the research published in those intervening years was much more sophisticated, and ". . .provided more support for the Machover theory, and for the use of human figure drawings as a diagnostic instrument." In drawing analysis, he considered global or overall ratings more reliable than those based on specific signs. If signs were to be used, he suggested that several drawings be obtained so that clinical judgment could be based on a larger sampling of drawing behavior.

Somewhat similar conclusions were reached by Roback (1968) in his review of the literature for the same time period, 1956-1967. While he, too, felt that global ratings were more reliable than those based on specific indicators, he was not as pleased as Swenson about the quality of research in that period. He stressed the need for standardized and validated scoring systems and emphasized that only competent future research would determine the specific uses of figure drawing tests.

Hammer (1959), in a critique of Swenson's 1957 review, claimed that Swenson misinterpreted the findings of several studies and was not familiar enough with Machover's work. In particular, he objected to Swenson's use of group comparisons, e.g., normals vs. other groups, since he felt group comparisons, on any variable, tend to obscure extreme occurrences which are clinically significant. Swenson's notion of the self, Hammer though, was quite unsophisticated. The self is complex and includes what we are, what we wish to be, and what we fear we might become.

Klopfer and Taulbee (1976), in a review of the literature from 1971 through 1974, concluded that drawings can only be regarded as "a suggestive kind of graphic behavior that will take on meaning as it is discussed with the subject and viewed in the context of other information." They felt that the problems with many of the studies they reviewed were due to the difficulty of inferring at a conscious level that which is an unconscious process.

34

Variations of the DAP

House-Tree-Person (HTP) Test was developed by Buck (1948, 1964) and advances in the technique were reviewed by Buck and Hammer (1969). In our review of the literature, we have included HTP studies but have concentrated on the person drawings. As the title of the test indicates, drawings of a house and a tree are requested in addition to that of a person. The developers of this technique maintain that the drawings of the house and tree dig deeper into the personality. Indeed, they have found that tree drawings are often the most revealing of all. A drawing scoring system has been developed and the authors advocate the use of color drawings and post-drawing questioning.

Chromatic or Color Drawings: Much of the work on the use of color in drawings has been done by developers and users of the House-Tree-Person Test (Buck, 1948, 1964; Hammer, 1953, 1969b, 1980; Jolles, 1971). Hammer maintains that color drawings reveal even more about the personality than pencil drawings. Hammer, Jolles and Precker (1950) have all talked about the significance of color. What follows is a brief summary of their findings:

Red – may be related to violence or excessive emotion; it has also been associated with cheerfulness; nursery level children who emphasized it are happier, well-adjusted, and more emotional in their personal reactions.
Yellow – suggestive of hostility, dependency, and infantile behavior. Yellow used with green to depict grass or a landscape is normal.
Orange – often suggests a good relationship with surroundings; may suggest areas of discomfort.
Blue – controlled reactions and self-restraint.
Green – blue and green are similar and represent controlled behavior. If much blue and green are used together, it indicates that the child feels secure as long as he is able to maintain control.
Black – controlled reactions, intellectual, compulsive.
Brown – timidity; may be used in times of regression. Brown and black used together suggest anxiety and depression.

When looking at the color in drawings, particular attention should be paid to excessive use of any one color. Sometimes excessive use of green, blue, or orange suggests a yearning for what the colors represent. Well-adjusted children use a variety of color in their pictures, while constricted and emotionally unstable chidren often use only a few.

35

Marzolf and Kirchner (1973) found that the significance of color is different for males and females. They suggest caution in inferring too much from color.

DAP and Questioning: To obtain more information about a drawing, a child may be questioned about it when the task is completed. Questions may be asked about any drawing, but the verbal responses are likely to be fuller and richer if the original drawing instructions are less specific. Children are more inclined to talk about drawings of *a* teacher, *a* doctor, *a* family, than about drawings of *your* teacher, *your* doctor, *your* family. "A" is less personal than "your" and its use reduces the chances of falsification. It is assumed, of course, that children will, in fact, be talking about their own teacher, their own doctor, their own family.

With some children, a request like "Tell me a story about your picture" will produce what the interpreter wants to know. Other children will require more prodding and more direct questioning about specific concerns. Some sample questions follow.

> For family drawings: How do this mother and father get along? How do the boy (girl) and his mother (father) get along? How does this boy (girl) get along with his (her) sisters and brothers? Do the mother and father love him (her) just as much as they love his (her) brothers and sisters? Which parent punishes the little boy?

> For school drawings: What does the little boy (girl) like best about school? What does he (she) hate most about school? Do other children like him (her)? Does this boy (girl) get along well with his (her) teacher? If he (she) could change school in some way, how would he (she) do it?

> For individual person drawings: Is the picture happy (unhappy)? What makes the boy (girl) unhappy? What makes him (her) happy? Does the boy (girl) like himself (herself)?

> For individual drawings of others (i.e. doctor, nurse, dentist): Is the doctor happy? Does he (she) like his patients? Does he (she) help people? Is he (she) in a hurry or does he (she) take his time?

DAP for Three- and Four-year-olds: Very young children are difficult to assess. They typically produce drawings with little detail, such as "tadpole" figures. These usually consist of a circle, with lines protruding from it and possibly some indication of eyes, nose or a mouth.

In addition to producing simple drawings, children at this age are often unable to understand the usual test instructions which are "Draw a picture of a person. You can draw any kind of person you want – a man or a woman or a boy or a girl." It is better in their case to gather several drawings, asking them to draw (one at a time) others they know well, like their mom, dad, sister or brother. Drawing analysis is then done by comparing the drawing of the self (which most children of this age are quite willing to do) with the drawings of the others. Any differences, omissions, emphases, etc. in the drawing of the self are considered significant.

DAP for Perceptually Impaired: Uhlin and Dickson (1970) compared two sets of drawings of spastic, cerebral-palsied children. In one set, children were required to draw HTP figures using a black crayon on white paper, while in the other, they were given a white crayon and black paper. The white-on-black drawings were significantly better in terms of detail, organization, form and relation of figure to ground. It seems that the perceptually handicapped find white paper backgrounds confusing and, when drawing on white, become easily disoriented with the form of the figure they are drawing.

The Self-Portrait: Berryman (1959) suggested an extension of drawing procedures by asking her subjects to "Draw a self-portrait, a picture of yourself." She used this in a battery along with drawings of a house, tree, person, and person of the opposite sex. She found it added extra information about the subject's self-concept and body-image. It was also useful in delineating the problem and planning the therapy.

Additional Persons: In several studies, drawings of figures in addition to that of the self or a person have been used to evaluate the personality of the drawer. Prytula et al. (1978) asked for drawings of a man, woman, and self in one study, and a man, woman, self, and Eskimo in another. In the first study, the drawing of the man was taller and erased more than the drawing of the self. The drawing of a man also contained more detail and body parts than that of a woman. In the second study, the drawing of the Eskimo was taller, wider, and greater in area than the drawing of a man or self. While there were more erasures in the drawing of the self than in that of the Eskimo, there were more body parts omitted from the Eskimo than from the other drawings. In neither study was an attempt made to examine the reasons for the differential treatment of the figures.

In an earlier study, Prytula and Hiland (1975) required their subjects to draw a man, a woman, and self. Fifth and sixth grade children drew the figure of the woman significantly taller and larger than the figure of the self. The authors speculated that this could indicate children's perceptions of dominant significant others in their lives, specifically the woman or symbolic mother.

In still another study, Prytula and Thompson (1973) compared adolescents' drawings of self, man, woman, and Eskimo. The Eskimo figure was drawn larger and wider and contained fewer erasures than the other three drawings. More omissions were found in the drawings of the woman and Eskimo than in the self or man. The investigators hypothesized that the relatively neutral, less familiar figure of the Eskimo may arouse less anxiety than the other figures, and this may account for its greater height, width, and area. Another explanation was that the attire of the Eskimo would increase its size and this could account for some of the expansiveness. Neither of these hypotheses was tested.

Dalby and Vale (1977), in a study comparing self-esteem with HFDs, instructed 115 fifth-graders to draw a picture of themselves and two friends of their own age. The three drawings were compared to find out if self-esteem was related to the relative size of figures. The size of the self figure relative to peer figures appeared unrelated to self-esteem. In this experiment, no attempt was made to find out the drawers' attitudes to or perceptions of their friends by further examining the drawings made of them.

The effects of different stimulus conditions on size variability on the DAP were investigated by Shanan (1962). Subjects were asked to draw a teacher, a person, and a person of the opposite sex. It was found that there was greater variability in the height of the three figures on the first administration than on the second administration six months later. While this study chose a teacher as a person in a specific social role, no attempt was made to examine the drawing in order to find out the subject's feelings about the teacher.

Draw-a-Person-in-the-Rain Test: Verinis, Lichtenberg, and Henrich (1974) adapted the DAP technique to measure the amount of stress a person was undergoing and how well he was able to deal with this stress without psychotic decompensation and regression. The subjects were asked to draw a person in the rain. The assumption was that the rain represented stress and that the quality of the rain drawn would indicate the amount of stress felt by the person. The person's defenses against stress would then be symbolized by the defenses drawn against the rain, e.g., an umbrella, coat or tree. While the Draw-a-Person-in-the-Rain Test may have some validity in the case of hospitalized psychiatric patients, it was not found useful for the general population.

The experimenters evaluated the drawings of 139 normal adolescents and found 49 percent of the drawings indicated neurosis, while 43 percent fell into the borderline psychotic category!

Draw-a-Car Test: Some researchers have substituted car drawings for HFDs. When Loney (1971) found that some children who refused to draw people liked to draw cars, she developed the Draw-a-Car Test as a method of studying enuresis and encopresis in children. Loney felt cars resemble people insofar as both are machines with nutritional-eliminative systems to accommodate fuel, store fuel, convert fuel to energy, and eliminate waste. Handler and Reyher (1964) also used a car in their drawing procedure, along with the drawings of male and female figures. Using the car, which they considered to be low in projective input as a comparison, they evaluated the projective factors, style, and quality of the HFDs.

Drawings of Animals: The meaning and significance of the drawings of animals were considered by Pustel, Sternlicht and De Respinis (1972). In examining the animal drawings of over 700 institutionalized retardates, more happy than unhappy drawings were found. The authors suggested the use of animal drawings for the study of personality.

Inside-of-the-Body Test: Tait and Ascher (1955) introduced a variation of the DAP Test which they called the Inside-of-the-Body Test. While the DAP focused mainly on the concept of physical exterior, the new test dealt with the concepts of what is inside the human body. The authors, both physicians, were curious about the development of these concepts and their possible distortions in illness. Subjects in their study were hospitalized psychiatric patients, candidates for admission to the Naval Academy, medically ill hospitalized patients without psychiatric problems, and a class of sixth grade students. They found that a higher-than-average percentage of medical and surgical patients drew the organ or system involved in the illness for which they were hospitalized. However, since Academy candidates in good health also emphasized a particular system in their drawings, the significance of this became less clear. The drawings of children and adults were different; adults dealt with various body systems in about the same frequency, while sixth graders typically omitted sexual organs and prominently emphasized the skeletomuscular system. Generally, all the drawings were anterior views which represented several anatomical items with an average of six to nine labels. The heart was the most frequently drawn organ and the gastrointestinal system was the most frequently represented system. The authors concluded that this test could be used as a screening tool in the investigation of psychosomatic problems.

In a study comparing children with congential heart problems with a group of normal children, Offord and Aponte (1970) administered the HTP, Sentence Completion, and Inside-of-the-Body Tests. While themes about health-illness were more prevalent in the congenital heart group on the HTP and Sentence Completion Tests, this group did not draw a greater number of hearts on the Inside-of-the-Body Test than the controls. They did draw relatively larger hearts and relatively fewer other organs. The investigators concluded that the body distortion of the congenital heart child pertains more to his perceptions of the inside of the body than to his view of the external body. They suggested that the Inside-of-the-Body Test be added to other projective tests investigating distortions of body image by the physically handicapped.

Brumback (1977) investigated the performance of 150 normal elementary school children on the Inside-of-the-Body Test. He found that a child initially perceives the interior of his body as composed mainly of heart, bones, hips, arms, and legs. As the normal child became older, he began to view the body as composed of many other internal organs and had a more exact idea of anatomic relationship of the body organs. Brumback viewed the Inside-of-the-Body Test as a potentially valuable adjunct in the psychological assessment of children, since it detected early any abnormalities in the development of the child's internal body perception. Further research was recommended to correlate Inside-of-the-Body Test results in children with various physical, emotional, or intellectual disorders.

Fifty adult patients with neuromuscular diseases were given the Inside-of-the-Body Test to examine the effect of a specific disability on test performance. The test was carried out by Brumback, Bertorini, and Liberman (1978) who found that the mean number of body parts identified in the drawings was 18. While some patients gave prominence to their diseased body structures, others omitted them. The authors noted that the patients showed greater body self-awareness than subjects evaluated 20 years ago.

Blum (1978) used drawings to study women's concepts of the anatomy of their sexual-reproductive organs. When 68 women, ages 20 through 78, were asked to draw their internal and external sexual organs, Blum found more than twice as many inadequate drawings as adequate ones. She attributed this lack of knowledge about the anatomy of the sexual organs to the physician's attitude toward women patients.

INSTRUCTIONS FOR ADMINISTRATION

Instructions for administering the human figure drawing test come in a number of variations. While they are all very similar, their slight differences may determine the kind of drawing produced. Some researchers have specified the drawing of a man or a woman or a boy or a girl. Others have asked for the drawing of a person in the rain. Still others, like Tait and Ascher (1955) whose major interest is in the inside-of-the-body, have instructed their subject to draw the inside of the body (including all of the organs), to draw a line from each organ to the outside and then to label that organ.

We believe that the less specific the instructions, the richer the drawings will be in terms of projective material. Here is our usual procedure: A child is given a sheet of letter-size paper (8½"x11") and a medium soft pencil, and is simply asked to *"draw a picture of a person."* If the child asks for more specific instructions or some kind of direction, the original instructions are repeated, or a non-directive type of remark is made indicating that he can draw any kind of person he wants. If the child draws only a part of the person, for example, the head, thank him for it and then ask him to draw a *whole* person. (The part of a person drawn may be significant. If a child draws only a head when requested to draw a person, he may be placing too much emphasis on this part of the body or it may be an area of concern. The head represents thinking proceeses, and this child may be concerned about mental adequacy.)

For a child who is very young or who does not understand what the word "person" means, the instructions should be repeated as follows:

"Draw a picture of a person. You can draw any kind of person you want – a man, or a woman, or a boy or a girl."

Never ask a child, "Can you draw a picture of a person?" Some children will refuse or deny that they are able to draw.

If a child draws the examiner, this should be noted. Insecure children often search for models to copy. What they may be saying is that they are not important enough to drawn (we assume most children draw themselves when asked to draw a picture of a person). These insecure children will draw others, such as examiners, teachers, parents, whom they view as more important than themselves.

When asking groups of children to draw, care should be taken to seat the children as far apart as possible to minimize copying. Again, it is the insecure child, lacking confidence in his own production, who is more likely to copy.

INTERPRETATION OF DRAWINGS

Once again the importance of using a multiple-measures approach must be emphasized. When assessing personality (or perceptions, values, attitudes), one should not use drawings in isolation, but along with other sources of information about the child.

When interpreting drawings, one should look at the *overall impression* the drawing gives and then look at specific signs, i.e., size, omissions, emphases, etc. The overall or global impression the drawing portrays or projects is more important than information given by one specific sign. One specific sign should not be viewed as indicative of a problem or concern. Several signs are required before inferences like that can be made about a child.

When we ask an individual to draw a person, we assume he is drawing himself. It is important to remember that sometimes a child draws his *physical* self. A child with a missing arm who draws a picture of a person with a missing arm is projecting his physical self into his drawing. It is a drawing of himself as he is. Other times, it is the *psychological* self which is projected into drawings. The psychological self is expressed through *wishes* or *symptoms* or *defenses*. If the child with a missing arm draws a picture of a person with two arms, he is expressing a *wish* which, in this case, is to have two arms. A physically intact child who draws a tiny picture of a person without arms may be expressing a *symptom* in his drawing. His drawing may indicate a fragile self-concept or difficulties in dealing with his environment. Yet another child may draw a picture of an overly confident person as a *defense* against feelings of insecurity.

It should be pointed out that a drawing represents what a person is like on the day he does the drawing. He may not have been like that yesterday, and we cannot predict how he will be in a month or two from now. Only by periodic collecting of his HFDs will we get some idea of a child's enduring or persistent characteristics.

Overall Impression

The first impression one receives from a drawing is important. One way of "getting into the drawing" is to put oneself in the position or stance represented in that drawing. This kinesthetic feedback should give some idea of overall affect. For example, a person drawn with hands on hips, his feet wide apart, and a cigarette in his mouth tends to give feelings of aggressivity, grandiosity, and expansiveness. On the other hand, a tiny drawing with arms at the side, knees together and ankles touching tends to portray shyness, constriction and perhaps a poor self-concept.

The overall affect of the drawing can be ascertained by looking at the drawing and asking questions such as:

Is the drawer likeable? Unlikeable?
Is he happy? Or sad?
Is he friendly? Unfriendly?
Does he get along well with others?
Is he carefree, calm or pleasant?
Is he uptight or tense?
Can he control his emotions or do they control him?
Is he active or energetic?
Is he passive or dull?
Is he strong? Weak?

The reader can probably think of other types of affect which could be deduced from a drawing.

Specific Signs

1. Size: Very large or very small drawings may be significant.

a) *Large drawings* that take up the entire page are often drawn by aggressive children with poorly developed inner controls. They are suggestive of grandiose feelings. Overactive, uninhibited children with poor controls overrun the boundaries of the page and have to leave off parts of the person. Occasionally, shy and timid children with poor self-concepts draw large figures, expressing the wish to be more powerful and noticeable.

b) *Small drawings,* one to two or three inches in height, are drawn by timid, shy, or withdrawn children and the small size reflects their insecurity. These children feel insignificant or tiny. Occasionally, overtly aggressive children with a poor self-image will draw small figures. While appearing aggressive and bold to the observer, inwardly these children are insecure and anxious.

2. Emphases and Exaggeration: Parts of the body that concern a child are often either *overemphasized* or *underemphasized.* Overemphasis may be seen through enlarging body parts, providing excessive detail of a body part, making the body part with a heavy line, etc. Underemphasis may be seen through making a body part smaller relative to other parts, lack of detail given to a part, or making a part with faint or sketchy lines.

a) *Heads* – both large and small heads are drawn by individuals who feel intellectually inadequate. Large heads are often seen in drawings of those who wish they were smarter or better able to achieve.

b) *Mouths* – either overemphasis or underemphasis of the mouth suggests a concern about this body part. Since the mouth is a major source of communication, children with language and speech disorders who are concerned about their handicap may enlarge the mouth or make it stand out more by heavy lining. Overly dependent children may also emphasize the mouth area.

c) *Eyes* – vacant eyes with no pupils may be drawn by children with visual processing learning problems.

d) *Arms* – large or long arms may be drawn by children who want to control or those who want strength and power. At times, large powerful arms are drawn by children with physical handicaps which affect their limbs. In these cases, the treatment given to the arms represents a wish to be more powerful. Small arms or faintly drawn arms are often drawn by children who fear power, who see themselves as weak and ineffective, and who perceive a lack of personal achievement. Often adolescent boys will draw muscular arms and muscular figures. This is due to their concerns about masculinity which are common at that age.

e) *Feet* – large feet are drawn by those who want security or a firm footing (security).

f) *Noses* – asthmatic children often enlarge or emphasize the nose because of their respiratory problems.

g) *Ears* – enlarged ears may be drawn by children with hearing problems. Some suspicious children, who perceive others as talking about them, may also emphasize the ears.

3. *Omissions:* Children concerned or anxious about specific body parts may omit them. Omissions are similar to underemphasis.

a) *Hands* – omission of the hands suggest insecurity and difficulty in dealing with the environment (home, school, people).

b) *Arms* – when arms are omitted, the child feels inadequate and ineffective. Since arms represent power and strength, their omission represents a perceived lack of power and strength.

c) *Legs* – legs provide support to the body; when they are omitted, the child perceives a lack of support and feels immobile.

d) *Feet* – when feet are omitted, the child may lack security and feel helpless.

e) *Nose* – the nose is often viewed as a symbol of power-striving and, if it is omitted, the child may feel powerless. Asthmatics may also omit the nose.

f) *Mouth* – omissions of this organ of communication may suggest

44

difficulty in relating to others. Some asthmatic children may omit mouths from their drawings.

4. *Teeth:* Teeth represent aggressiveness. While some aggression may be considered normal, teeth may represent abnormal aggressivity.

5. *Sex Organs:* When sex organs are drawn, they may be considered indicators of aggressiveness. Actually, we have often noticed genitals in the drawings of four- to six-year-old children whose parents have walked around the house nude to help their offspring develop a healthy attitude toward their bodies. However, Koppitz (1968), who often found genitals in the drawings of severely disturbed children, relates genitals to acute body anxiety and poor impulse control.

6. *Buttons – Belly Button:* Buttons represent dependency and are often drawn by young children up to the age of six or seven. This is normal since they are dependent on their parents. The belly button represents the early dependency on the umbilical cord. Buttoning is one of the more difficult tasks in early childhood, and many children are forced to rely on their mother's help. After age six or seven, the inclusion of buttons on the drawings may suggest too much dependency.

7. *Sun:* When the sun is included in a child's picture, it is usually representative of parental love and support. The sun is a source of warmth, as are nurturing parents. At times, clouds may block or hide the sun. If this is the case, there is a possibility the child is not receiving parental love.

8. *Mouth Treatment (smile-frown):* Happy or sad faces may reflect happy or sad people.

9. *Unusual Ways of Drawing People:*
   a) *Stick Figures* – these figures are often drawn by children who are reluctant to reveal themselves. They want to be safe and avoid all risk-taking. When stick figures are produced, they are accepted, but the child is asked to draw another figure which is not a stick figure.
   b) *Cowboys* – cowboys are drawn by children who want to be masculine and tough.
   c) *Clowns* – clowns are often drawn by children with poor self-concepts and self-depreciating thoughts.
   d) *Monsters and Witches* – these figures are drawn by children with very poor self-concepts and feelings of depersonalization.

45

10. *Poorly Integrated Figures:* Poor integration refers to figures in which the head, arms and legs do not join the body or where hands do not join the arms, etc. These figures may be drawn by children with motoric types of learning disability and/or those who are doing poorly in school.

11. *Erasures:* Some erasing is normal if it improves the drawing. However, excessive erasing without improvement of the drawing is related to anxiety and uncertainty. At times a particular body part is erased. This is the part which is of concern to the drawer. If the entire figure is erased, the anxiety is likely more generalized.

12. *Shading:* Shading refers to pencil strokes which are designed to fill in an area as in coloring or darkening a shirt, or in illuminating the contour of the body. Shading is always related to anxiety. If all the body is shaded (some disturbed children even shade the face), the anxiety may be considered as generalized overall anxiety. If only a specific body part is shaded, then the anxiety may be related to that part.

13. *Line Pressure:* Heavy line pressure is often associated with aggressive, forceful, high-energy individuals. Light line pressure may be indicative of low energy, inhibition, and shyness. Generally, boys tend to use heavier pressure than girls.

14. *Baselining and Placement on the Bottom Edge of the Paper:* Children requiring security or support will often draw a line or grass under their figures. The line is a base which provides them with a firm footing. Other children in need of support and security will draw their figure at the bottom of the page with feet touching the bottom edge.

15. *Slanting Figure:* Slanted figures (slanted more than 15° from the vertical) are suggestive of feelings of imbalance, and the lacking of a secure footing. The drawing seems on the verge of falling over, creating a toppling feeling.

16. *Placement of Figure on the Page:* Where a child places his figure may be significant. Placement near the top or high on a page suggests that the drawer may use fantasy to achieve goals or may, in fact, be striving for achievement or finding it difficult to reach goals. Placement near the bottom or low on the page may indicate insecurity or a person who is reality-oriented. Left-side placement suggests an orientation towards the past, while right-side placement is more future-oriented.

Examples of Drawings
Measuring
Personality

DRAWING 1: "You better believe I'm tough"

The Drawer
Boy, 10 years old; above average ability; behavior problem in school, particularly acting out in class.

The Projection
Overall Impression: Boldness, aggression, defiance, masculinity, grandiose feelings
Specific Indicators:
- Very large figure (aggressive with poor inner control)
- Enlarged mouth, gun (more signs of aggressivity)
- Hands-on-hips stance (defiance)
- Hair emphasis (masculinity)
- Drawing runs off page, no room for feet (shows overactive, uninhibited, impulsive tendencies)

DRAWING 2: ". . . nobody knows I'm
there at all"

The Drawer
   Boy, 14 years old; mildly retarded; requires
   special education but, since none is available
   to him, has to attend regular class in which
   he always places last.

The Projection
   Overall Impression: Insignificance, shyness,
   smallness.
   Specific Indicators:
      • Very small figure (reflects insecurity felt
        by shy, timid or withdrawn child)
      • Baselining, i.e., feet touching bottom of
        page (shows need for security and sup-
        port)
      • Large head (concern about intellectual
        adequacy)
      • Large ears (concern about what others
        are saying about him)

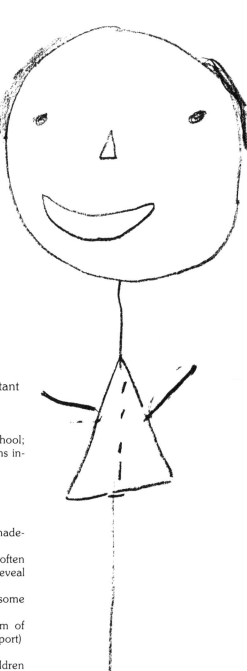

DRAWING 3: "You are more important than I am"

The Drawer
   Boy, eight years old; doing poorly in school; although IQ is average, motor problems interfere with learning.

The Projection
   Overall Impression: Head dominance
   Specific Indicators:
   - Large head (feels intellectually inadequate, wishes to achieve more)
   - Partial stick figure (stick figures are often drawn by those reluctant to reveal themselves)
   - Erasures with no improvement (some anxiety about arms and hands)
   - Baselining, i.e., feet touch bottom of page (in need of security and support)
   - No hands (poor achiever)
   - Child drew examiner (insecure children often search for a model to copy because of their lack of confidence)

51

DRAWING 4: "I can't do what they want
me to"

The Drawer
  Boy, nine years old; average IQ but has
  learning disabilities; parents disappointed
  with school performance.

The Projection
  Overall Impression: Head deemphasis
  Specific Indicators:
    • Tiny head (feels intellectually inade-
      quate)
    • Short arms (feels weak, ineffective and
      lacking in personal achievement)

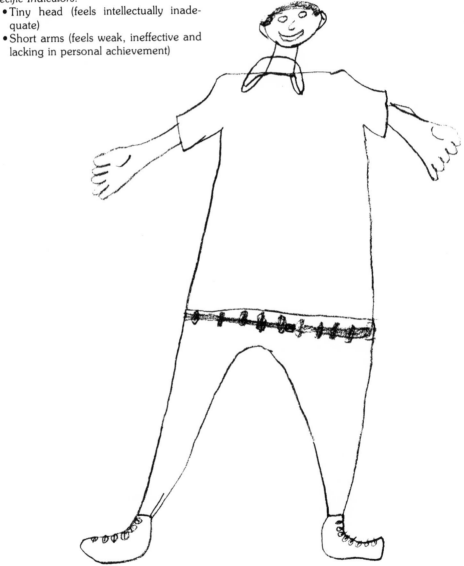

DRAWING 5: "I wish I didn't talk so funny"

The Drawer
Girl, 12 years old; IQ in slow-learning range; in special class; speech and language problems are her greatest deficit.

The Projection
Overall Impression: Head dominance, helplessness
Specific Indicators:
- Large head (feels intellectually inadequate and wishes she could do better)
- Enlarged mouth (concerned about her handicap)
- Buttons (suggests she is overdependent)
- Small hands or no arms (feels helpless about inability to achieve)

DRAWING 6: "It's scary when I can't breathe."

The Drawer
   Boy, nine years old; superior intelligence; asthmatic; behavior problem at home and in school; parents and teachers concerned.

The Projection
   Overall Impression: Instability and lack of balance
   Specific Indicators:
   • Large nose (asthmatic children often emphasize the nose because of their respiratory problems)
   • Mouth omission (also often found in asthmatic children's drawings)
   • Eyes directed to area of concern?
   • Slanting figure (suggests feelings of imbalance)
   • Baselining (suggests insecurity)

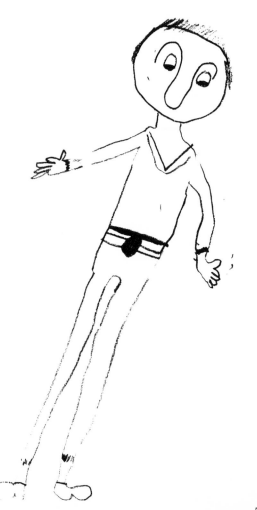

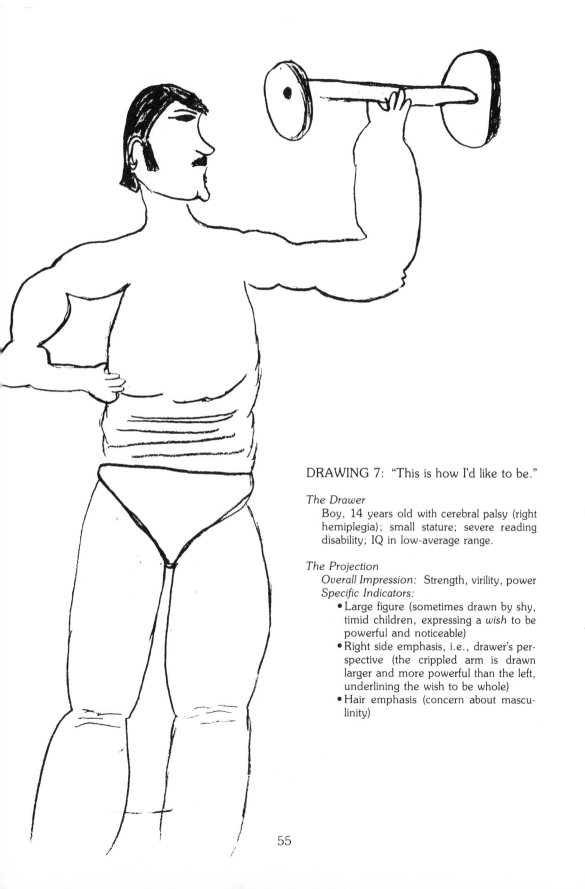

DRAWING 7: "This is how I'd like to be."

The Drawer
  Boy, 14 years old with cerebral palsy (right hemiplegia); small stature; severe reading disability; IQ in low-average range.

The Projection
  Overall Impression: Strength, virility, power
  Specific Indicators:
  • Large figure (sometimes drawn by shy, timid children, expressing a *wish* to be powerful and noticeable)
  • Right side emphasis, i.e., drawer's perspective (the crippled arm is drawn larger and more powerful than the left, underlining the wish to be whole)
  • Hair emphasis (concern about masculinity)

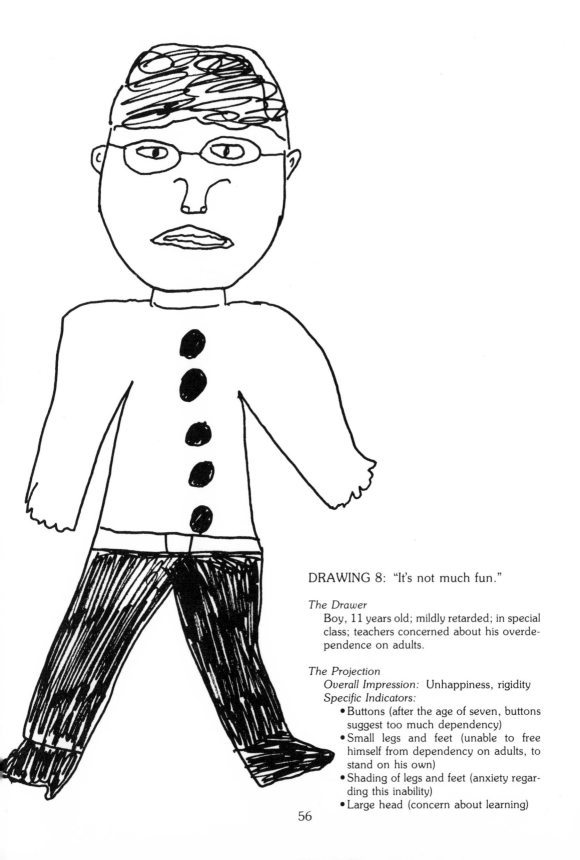

DRAWING 8: "It's not much fun."

The Drawer
Boy, 11 years old; mildly retarded; in special class; teachers concerned about his overdependence on adults.

The Projection
Overall Impression: Unhappiness, rigidity
Specific Indicators:
- Buttons (after the age of seven, buttons suggest too much dependency)
- Small legs and feet (unable to free himself from dependency on adults, to stand on his own)
- Shading of legs and feet (anxiety regarding this inability)
- Large head (concern about learning)

56

DRAWING 9: "I just can't figure it out!"

The Drawer
Girl, six years old; average ability; learning problems, e.g., difficulty in locating various parts of the body and in distinguishing left from right.

The Projection
Overall Impression: Poor body image
Specific Indicators:
- Head undifferentiated from body (has not yet developed concept of what body is like)
- Peculiarly-shaped arms (cannot "image" parts of body)
- Eye emphasis (concern about eye-hand coordination)

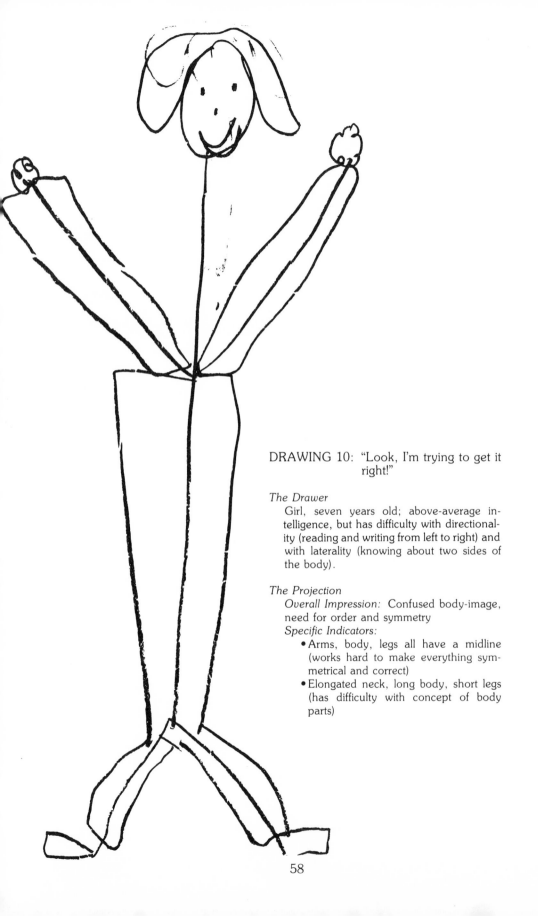

DRAWING 10: "Look, I'm trying to get it right!"

The Drawer
   Girl, seven years old; above-average intelligence, but has difficulty with directionality (reading and writing from left to right) and with laterality (knowing about two sides of the body).

The Projection
   Overall Impression: Confused body-image, need for order and symmetry
   Specific Indicators:
      • Arms, body, legs all have a midline (works hard to make everything symmetrical and correct)
      • Elongated neck, long body, short legs (has difficulty with concept of body parts)

DRAWING 11: "Boy, is this world confusing!"

The Drawer
Boy, six years old in kindergarten; average
ability but with learning and behavior problems; motor problems predominate.

The Projection
Overall Impression: Confusion, dissociation
Specific Indicators:
- Lack of integration of body parts, i.e.,
  legs not joined to body, head drawn
  separately (often seen in drawings of
  children with motor problems)
- Devil's head (monster-like figures are
  often drawn by children with poor self-
  concept; also, subject sometimes
  behaves "like a devil")

59

DRAWING 12: "If only I could catch a
ball."

The Drawer
Boy, six years old; average intelligence, but
doing poorly in grade one; gross-motor
problems, i.e., difficulty in moving arms and
legs efficiently, interferes with learning.

The Projection
Overall Impression: Awkwardness, a feeling
of progress being impeded

Specific Indicators:
- Enlarged feet (need for security or firm
  footing; also may symbolize motor
  problems which prevent free movement)
- Shading of feet (indication of anxiety
  regarding his problem in this area)
- Enlarged arm (he wishes he could have
  a strong well-coordinated arm to catch
  a ball, etc.)

60

DRAWING 13: "Why can't I read like
other kids?"

The Drawer
Boy, 10 years old; average intelligence but
with visual processing disabilities which
obstruct learning, i.e., letters often appear
upside down, or reversed or running
together.

The Projection
Overall Impression: Immobility
Specific Indicators:
• Vacant non-seeing eyes (these are often
drawn by children with visual process-
ing problems)
• Baselining, i.e., drawing on bottom
edge of paper (in need of security and
support)
• Feet omitted (insecurity)

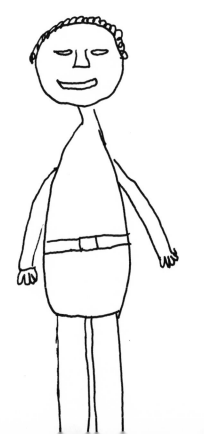

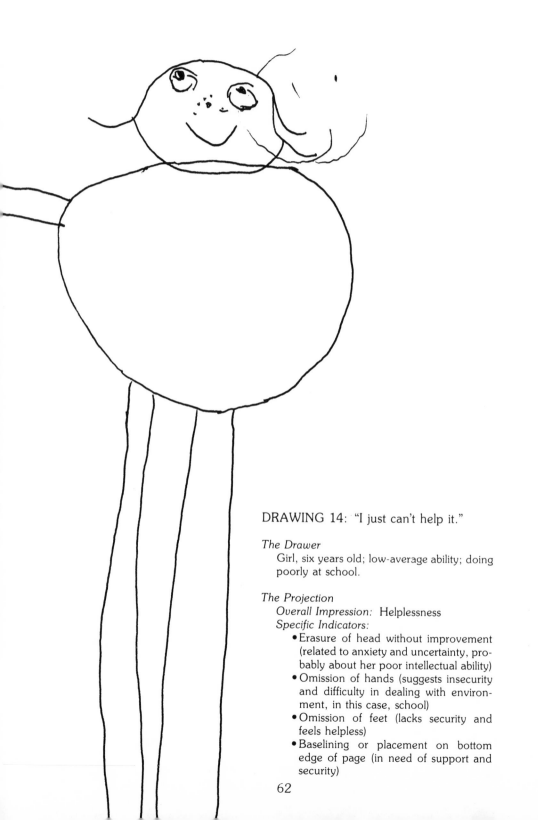

DRAWING 14: "I just can't help it."

The Drawer
Girl, six years old; low-average ability; doing poorly at school.

The Projection
Overall Impression: Helplessness
Specific Indicators:
- Erasure of head without improvement (related to anxiety and uncertainty, probably about her poor intellectual ability)
- Omission of hands (suggests insecurity and difficulty in dealing with environment, in this case, school)
- Omission of feet (lacks security and feels helpless)
- Baselining or placement on bottom edge of page (in need of support and security)

62

DRAWING 15: "Everybody hates me and
I hate myself."

The Drawer

Boy, 13 years old; slow learner; severe reading disability; difficulty getting along with peers at school; abandoned by mother, raised by relatives; burning accident during infancy resulted in physical deformities, i.e. claw-like hands.

The Projection

Overall Impression: Self-depreciation

Specific Indicators:

• Clown figure (often drawn by children with poor self-concepts and self-depreciating thoughts)

• Teeth (aggressiveness or belligerence, does not know how else to deal with his situations)

• Belly button (represents early dependency on umbilical cord; child missed bonding with mother and has not developed a confident independence)

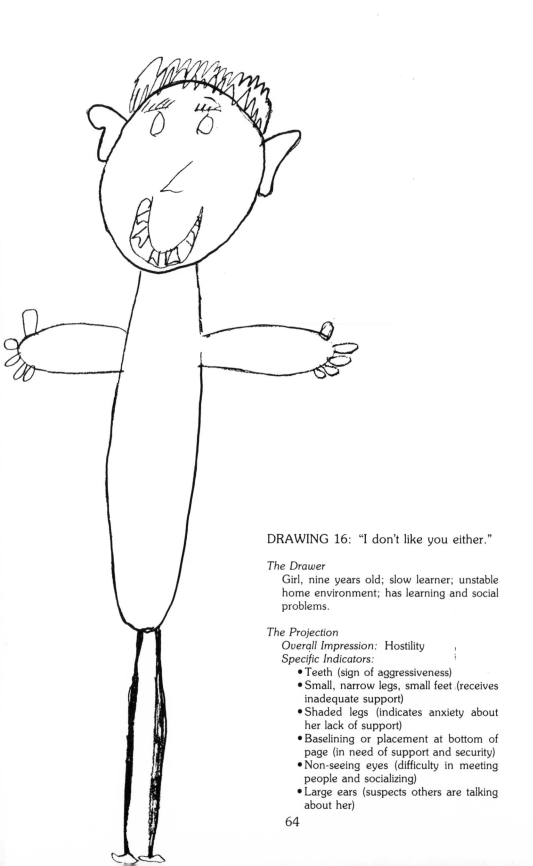

DRAWING 16: "I don't like you either."

The Drawer
Girl, nine years old; slow learner; unstable home environment; has learning and social problems.

The Projection
Overall Impression: Hostility
Specific Indicators:
- Teeth (sign of aggressiveness)
- Small, narrow legs, small feet (receives inadequate support)
- Shaded legs (indicates anxiety about her lack of support)
- Baselining or placement at bottom of page (in need of support and security)
- Non-seeing eyes (difficulty in meeting people and socializing)
- Large ears (suspects others are talking about her)

DRAWING 17: "They're talking about
me."

The Drawer
Girl, 10 years old; slow learner; doing
poorly at school; perceives others as dislik-
ing her.

The Projection
Overall impression: Unusual drawing
Specific Indicators:
- Large ears (since she has no hearing
  problem, this indicates she suspects
  people talk about her)
- Shading of ears (indicates anxiety about
  her suspicions)
- Wrinkled forehead (worried?)
- No hands (suggests insecurity and dif-
  ficulty dealing with school and people)
- Head enlarged (concern about intellec-
  tual adequacy)

DRAWING 18: "I feel like showing off."

The Drawer
 Boy, five years old; average ability; seen at
 preschool screening.

The Projection
 Overall Impression: Unusual drawing
 Specific Indicators:
 - Penis (could indicate aggressiveness or
   body anxiety, or merely that he has
   often seen his father in the nude)
 - Belly button (sign of dependency but
   often seen in drawings of children this
   age)
 - Wing-like arms or hands (concern
   about relating to the environment?)

DRAWING 19: "I wish I were smart and had friends."

The Drawer

Boy, five years old; average ability but with social-emotional problems; learning difficulties in kindergarten.

The Projection

Overall Impression: Head disproportion

Specific Indicators:

- Very large head (feels intellectually inadequate, wishes to be smarter)
- Large ears (sometimes drawn by suspicious children who think others talk about them)
- Shading on ears and body (related to anxiety)
- Buttons (sign of dependency)
- Baselining, i.e., drawn standing on something (needs security and support)

DRAWING 20: "I feel sad."

The Drawer
    Boy, nine years old; above-average ability; school performance poor; unhappy in class; has fine- and gross-motor learning problems.

The Projection
    Overall Impression: Unhappiness
    Specific Indicators:
- Frown (he is miserable)
- Foot emphasis (wants a firm footing or security which he does not have; also has gross motor problems and is clumsy)
- Arms in different directions (they do not perform well for him)
- Hands omission (suggests insecurity and difficulty in dealing with environment, in this case, school)

DRAWING 21: "Why am I so dumb?"

The Drawer
    Boy, 11 years old; in slow-learning range;
always at bottom of class.

The Projection
    Overall Impression: Head emphasis
    Specific Indicators:
- Large head (feels intellecually inadequate)
- Draws head only, even when asked to
draw a person a second time (the wish
and need to be smarter supersede all
other needs)

DRAWING 22: "Why can't I go home?"

The Drawer
    Boy, eight years old; above-average ability; removed from parents due to family instability.

The Projection
    Overall Impression: Hopelessness
    Specific Indicators:
        • Upper left-hand corner placement (feels hopeless about reaching goal, in his case, to have a family; also suggests anxiety)
        • Buttons (sign of dependency, in this case a wish to be dependent on someone)
        • Erasures without improvement (indicates anxiety and uncertainty)

DRAWING 23: "I want to grow up to be
              strong like this."

The Drawer
    Boy, 14 years old; average intelligence; no
    marked social-emotional or learning prob-
    lems.

The Projection
    Overall Impression: Strength, masculinity,
    aggression
    Specific Indicators:
        • Muscled parts of body (often drawn by
          adolescent boys who are usually con-
          cerned about masculinity during this
          stage of their lives)
        • Hair emphasis (masculinity)
        • Clenched fist (aggression)

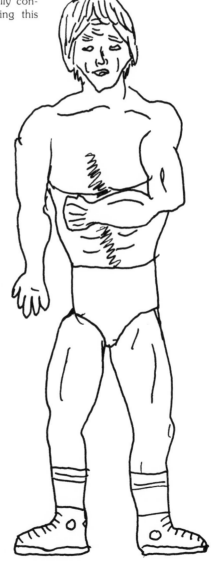

The Drawer
A 12-year-old native boy; borderline intelligence in special class.

The Projection
Overall Impression: Aggression, masculin-
ity, a picture with conflicting messages.
Specific Indicators:
- Cowboy figures (drawn by children who
  wish to be masculine and tough)
- Guns (symbols of aggression)
- Sun (usually represents parental love
  and support)
- Dead trees (sometimes drawn by
  disturbed persons)
- Environment (in spite of the presence of
  the sun, there are "hostile" elements
  too, like clouds, snakes, dead trees and
  guns)
- Self seen as victim? (he has been
  disarmed)
- Faces (these are more white than Indian)

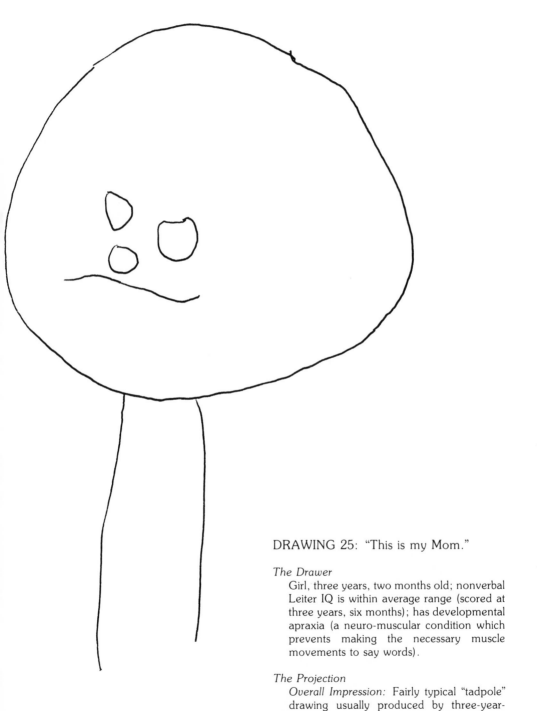

DRAWING 25: "This is my Mom."

The Drawer
   Girl, three years, two months old; nonverbal
   Leiter IQ is within average range (scored at
   three years, six months); has developmental
   apraxia (a neuro-muscular condition which
   prevents making the necessary muscle
   movements to say words).

The Projection
   Overall Impression: Fairly typical "tadpole"
   drawing usually produced by three-year-
   olds.

74

DRAWING 26: "This is Freda."

The Drawer
Same as #25. This little girl is receiving regular speech therapy at a university clinic; she can say 18 approximations of words and points to identify the person she has drawn; Freda is her speech therapist.

The Projection
Overall Impression: Fairly typical "tadpole" drawing usually produced by three-year-olds.

75

DRAWING 27: "This is myself."

The Drawer
Same as #25 and #26. This little girl's parents are interested in helping their daughter and wonder whether or not she is *concerned about her handicap.*

The Projection
Overall Impression: The drawing of the self is different from the others.
Specific Indicators:
- Mouth emphasis (children with speech and language handicaps often enlarge the mouth or make it stand out by heavy lining as this child did – she is concerned about her handicap)
- Mouth difference (drawn differently from Mom's and Freda's)
- Nose omission (feels powerless)

76

CHAPTER 5

DRAWINGS AS A
MEASURE OF SELF IN
RELATION TO OTHERS

RESEARCH TO DATE

The Draw-a-Family (DAF) Technique

The family drawing technique was first suggested by Hulse (1951). In his study, emotionally disturbed children were asked: "Will you draw your family (for me)?" When finished, the children were asked to identify the figures and to say whatever they wanted about their drawings. In evaluating the drawings, Hulse took into consideration size of the figures, their relation to each other expressed in relative size, and their distance and distribution over the paper. However, he was more concerned with the total drawing. He pointed out that while attention was paid to details such as the strength of the pencil stroke, shading and coloring, the sequence in which the family members appeared, the cartoon-like exaggerations of certain persons or body features, and the omission of others, it was the general concept or Gestalt of the picture which was the main source of early information about the child's conflicts and which gave diagnostic value to the method.

Hulse believed that family drawings gave insight into a child's perception of the family constellation, the amount of resolution of the Oedipus conflict and the child's concept of himself, his anxieties, and his fantasies.

The drawings of normal chldren were also used by Hulse (1952) to determine how family conflicts might be projected. Using his Gestalt approach, he was able to determine some developmental conflicts of childhood. He concluded that normal children project their deeper emotional feelings and attitudes toward different family members into their drawings.

The validity of the DAF technique was investigated by Deren (1975), since Hulse's reports were mainly of a clinical nature and contained little information on construct validity. Deren studied the family drawings of 239 members of families, including drawings made by both children and adults. The drawings of black, Puerto Rican, and white groups were scored for size, detail, and number of figures. Ethnicity was related to significant differences on the size variable. Blacks, for example, drew a larger mother figure than the other groups. Quite often, the family drawn was not the same size as the child's actual family. This was particularly true of two-member families, who typically produced more than two figures. The author concluded that, in general, his findings supported the validity of the DAF technique.

The family drawings of black and white children were compared by Reznikoff and Reznikoff (1956). Sex differences were greater than racial differences. The boys placed themselves in the center of the group and omitted the mother figure significantly more often than the girls. The productions of black and white groups were similar, but black children more frequently omitted figures and excluded siblings. It was noted too that children from lower-income families did not include the mother in their drawings, made an older sibling the largest member, drew families as if suspended in air, and frequently represented the father figure without arms.

Lawton and Sechrest (1962) analyzed the family drawings of 61 boys from homes with a father and 58 boys from fatherless homes. The drawings were scored with reference to the size of the parents, the positon of the son in relation to the father, the detail present in the drawing of the father and the degree of spontaneity with which the father was drawn. No differences were found between the drawings of father-absent and father-present boys.

An adaptation and extension of Hulse's technique were devised by Shearn and Russell (1970). Instead of asking the subject to draw his own family, the authors asked him to draw a family. Drawings were obtained from one or both parents, as well as from the child. A comparison of parental drawings with the child's provided the authors with clues regarding the important aspects of family dynamics. Shearn and Russell used case studies to illustrate the significance of these drawings.

Britain (1970) found that stress had an effect on the family drawings of four- and five-year-olds. In comparison to the drawings of controls, the productions of children subjected to stress were constricted, grossly distorted, disorganized, fragmented, and poor in line quality. Britain concluded that dynamic defensive processes were reflected in drawings.

Koppitz (1968) believed that children's drawings of a family reflected their attitude toward their family. She said, "On a drawing, a child can reveal unconsciously negative attitudes toward his family by disguising the shapes of his parents and siblings and by using signs and symbols he himself may not be aware of." Her instructions for obtaining the family portrait were, "I would like you to draw a picture of your whole family; you can draw it any way you want to." In drawing analysis, omissions of family members, substitutions, and the size and position of figures were considered important.

Di Leo (1973) saw family drawings as diagnostic aids in the search for the causes of behavior disorders. He found a strong affective component in these drawings, which revealed the child's feelings in relation to significant family members. In appraising the drawings, he considered the following to be significant: omission of a family member; omission of self; the parent figure the child placed himself closest to; similarity in style or clothing to another member; role in the family; and interaction and isolation. Di Leo considered Kinetic Family Drawings useful for older children who could portray movement and recommended this procedure after first obtaining the drawing of a family.

The Kinetic Family Drawing (KFD) Technique

The Kinetic Family Drawing technique was introduced by Burns and Kaufman (1970). The instructions for administration differ from those of akinetic techniques: "Draw a picture of everyone in your family, including you, doing something. Try to draw whole people, not cartoons or stick people. Remember, make everyone doing something – some kind of action." The analysis of KFDs was focused on action or movement rather than on inert figures. Styles such as compartmentalization or underlining were considered suggestive of unstable homes. Actions portraying mothers cooking and fathers reading the newspaper were considered positive, while actions portraying the mother cleaning or ironing and the father driving to work or cutting the lawn were considered negative. Rivalry in families was depicted by forceful action among family members, like throwing a ball or a knife. The KFD technique was based on the authors' clinical experience. No formal evidence of reliability or validity was provided.

In a later volume, Burns and Kaufman (1972) present a more detailed scoring system in which special attention is given to the various KFD symbols. They include a scoring manual and a grid and analysis sheet to assist the interpreter. The following are considered in scoring: styles such as compartmentalization, encapsulation and edging; symbols; actions of individual figures; actions between individual figures; characteristics such as erasures, arm extensions, omission of body parts, and omission of figures; height of the individual figures; and distance of the child from the mother and father.

Sims (1974) compared the findings from KFDs with the results of the Family Relations Indicator (FRI), a standardized picture projective technique for investigating the relationships between family members. When 100 emotionally disturbed children were tested, it was found that the drawings and the results from the FRI were significantly related for the mother and father figure but not for siblings. Sims concluded that KFDs are a valid technique in the study of disturbed parental relations.

Schornstein and Derr (1978) found KFDs most useful in child abuse cases. However, they asked the parents, not the children, to do the drawing! What they produced was helpful in assessing family relationships, determining how abused children are regarded by their parents, finding out who perpetrates the abuse, and evaluating whether or not the abuse has developed as a reaction to situational pressures.

A study by McPhee and Wenger (1976) showed lack of support for the basic interpretation of KFD styles. Burns and Kaufman considered KFD styles suggestive of defensiveness and indicated that styles such as compartmentalization, lining on the bottom of figures, edging and encapsulation were reflected in the drawings of severely disturbed children. McPhee and Wenger compared the KFDs of emotionally disturbed children attending a special school with those of normals. The KFDs were scored for style in a reliable fashion by five judges. The results confirmed the existence of KFD styles. However, style was not predominantly associated with the disturbed sample. As a matter of fact, it was more evident in the KFDs of well-adjusted children.

In a study by Levenberg (1975), doctoral clinicians, predoctoral interns, and hospital secretaries judged 36 children to be normal or disturbed on the basis of KFDs, indicating their degree of confidence in each rating. All doctoral level clinicians and almost all of the intern group were found to perform better than chance, and the findings suggested that the KFD appeared to be a valid measure.

A comparison of the KFDs of 50 early childhood youngsters with perceptual motor delays with 50 normals was undertaken by Raskin and Pitcher-Baker (1977). The drawings of the children with delayed development showed more isolation rejection and body concerns than those of normal children. The authors found KFDs valuable for the diagnosis and treatment of the problems of young children.

Jacobson (1973) identified and described the characteristics of normal primary school-aged children's KFDs. She found elevated figures, lining at the bottom of figures, omission of body parts, and the sun often enough in the drawings of normal children to convince her they were invalid emotional indicators. The characteristics, styles, symbols, and actions described by Burns and Kaufman were so infrequent that the author concluded they were likely indicators of maladjustment.

Mangum (1975) found the KFD technique most useful for assessing familial identification in 10- to 12-year-old mentally retarded children. The drawings of 90 black, Anglo and Chicano youngsters revealed identification with a specific family member. There were no differences among the three groups and between the sexes in their identification pattern.

Scoring is never the easiest part of any technique. The KFD system is no exception, and several researchers have tried to make it more objective for the benefit of scorers. O'Brien and Patton (1974) devised a system by comparing children's drawings with their scores on the Coopersmith Self-Esteem Inventory, the Children's Manifest Anxiety Scale, and a School Behavior Checklist completed by their teachers. The KFDs were analyzed for manifest anxiety, general self-concept, school and academic self-concept, aggressive behavior, withdrawal behavior, and hostile behavior. The results suggested that the most important variable for predicting manifest anxiety was the activity level of the father! For school and academic self-concept, the most important variable was the number of figures in the drawing. The larger the family drawn, the greater the concept.

A quick scoring guide for the interpretation of KFDs was developed by Reynolds (1978). Listing 32 potentially significant anxiety indicators gleaned from a review of the literature, he discussed their meanings. He also pointed out the pros and cons of this guide.

Myers (1978) developed a quantitative scoring system to score 21 measurable styles, actions, and characteristics of KFDs. The system was used to evaluate the drawings obtained from four groups of boys and to test its effectiveness in differentiating among two levels of emotional adjustment and two age levels. Myers' results generally supported the feasibility of using this scoring system to differentiate the emotionally disturbed from the emotionally well-adjusted. The system was also, in part, sensitive to some age differences, but the investigator cautioned against its use for this purpose.

The Draw-a-Group (DAG) Technique

Groups other than the family have been used to assess self in relation to others. Hare and Hare (1956) devised the Draw-a-Group Test to reveal the structure of a group and the individual's adjustment to it. Here are the instructions for the test:

> Think of the children you like to play with most on the playground. Now think of the things you like to do best with this group of children. Then draw a picture of your group doing the thing you like to do best. When you are through, we will write down what is going on in your picture.

An exploratory study in 10 elementary school classrooms compared the teachers' rankings of the children's status in class with the drawing results. The correlation obtained was significant. However, the authors realized that more studies were needed before this approach could be used with confidence.

In a study by Cohen, Money, and Uhlenhuth (1972), selected features of self-and-others drawings were examined to determine (relative to age, height, and sex) the differences in the heights of figures drawn. The subjects were first asked to draw a picture of themselves and their best friend, and then to draw self with the examiner. While the subjects did represent the difference between the height of self and the height of the examiner, they did not draw themselves small enough.

Mott (1954) compared four- and five-year-old children's drawings of mother, father, and child. She found that the children drew the mother taller than themselves and a little shorter than the father. Greater attention to detail was found in the drawings of the mother and she was most often placed in the center of the family.

The Kinetic School Drawing (KSD) Technique

A variation of the KFD, the Kinetic School Drawing (KSD), was developed by Prout and Phillips (1974) to find out how children perceive themselves in the school situation. Subjects were given the following instructions:

> I'd like you to draw a school picture. Put yourself, your teacher, and a friend or two in the picture. Make everyone doing something. Try to draw whole people and make the best drawing you can. Remember, draw yourself, your teacher, and a friend too, and make everyone doing something.

In evaluating the drawing, the child's perceptions of himself in school, of his teacher, and of his peers were taken into consideration. While the authors felt their approach had potential, no evidence regarding validity has been provided and no systematized scoring system formulated.

Schneider (1977) used procedures known as multiple regression to find out if a *combination* of the KSD score, KFD score, age and IQ significantly predicted the family and school ratings which he had done beforehand. He found that neither the KSD score nor the KFD score added significantly to the level of prediction achieved by age and IQ alone. While the overall results of his study offered little support for KSDs, Schneider did not feel that they proved the technique to be useless. He recommended more research into scoring procedures and suggested that the criteria used should be more sensitive to the degree of difference rather than to the mere presence or absence of a characteristic. He viewed a subject's perception of self and perception of his relationships as being the most directly related to KSD responses.

Akinetic School Drawing Techniques

In another effort to obtain information about a child's perception of school, Kutnick (1978) asked elementary school children to "draw me a picture of a classroom with people in it." When the drawings were finished, the children were questioned about the content of their pictures. Drawing analysis focused on human figures, the classroom and classroom objects, and the teacher; also, certain aspects of what the child had said were correlated with what he had drawn. At six years of age over 90 percent of the children drew a teacher, but only 22 percent perceived the teacher as an authority figure or a disciplinarian. By nine years of age, 85 percent of the children drew a teacher and 60 percent perceived the teacher as a disciplinarian. Kutnick concluded that drawings throw light on the teacher's social position in school. He also found more kinetic or action drawings between ages nine and ten, suggesting that at this age children are more aware of social roles of both pupil and teacher.

Lourenso, Greenberg, and Davidson (1965) were interested in relating differences in personality traits, such as self-image, parent image, compliance, and work orientation, to differences in academic achievement. They divided their subjects, lower socioeconomic status black children, into three groups on the basis of achievement on a reading test: "good achiever," "average achievers," and "poor achievers." The children were asked to draw two pictures, one of "My

Family" and a second of "A Child in School." They were also told to circle themselves in the family drawing. (We do not recommend this procedure, since valuable information may be lost if you tell children to circle themselves. If children spontaneously circle or encapsulate themselves, they gave us a valuable clue about their perceptions of self with others.) The three achievement groups were not appreciably different, but when achievement level and sex were considered together, clear-cut differences emerged. The most striking finding was the extent to which poor achieving boys differed from all the others in showing low self-esteem. Their self-drawings were often incomplete, lacking hands, head disproportionate to the body, inappropriately clothed, and with unhappy facial expressions. All girls showed a more positive attitude to school by depicting more work and school content in their drawings. As to following instructions, good achievers of both sexes did this well. Their family drawings, however, tended to be restricted to the bare minimum or poor in detail. In fact, only seven percent of the good-achieving girls added extra content and objects to their drawings, in contrast to 88 percent of the poor-achieving boys.

INSTRUCTIONS FOR ADMINISTRATION

Group drawings may be of two kinds – *akinetic* and *kinetic*. The akinetic kind was the first to be used. Children were just asked to draw a family or some other group. The instructions specified the *kind* of group to be drawn, i.e., family, classroom group, friends, but did not tell the drawer *how* to draw a group. More recently, children have been asked to draw a group *doing something* and to *include themselves* (and sometimes others) in the drawing. In other words, they were asked for a *kinetic* drawing.

The kind of drawing obtained depends on the instructions. When children are asked to draw a group, they will probably produce an akinetic or non-movement drawing. When asked to draw a group *doing something*, they will make a drawing portraying movement, a kinetic drawing. Since akinetic instructions are less specific, children are free to produce any kind of drawing they want. They may include themselves or not, as they please. They may put anyone they want into the picture. They may organize the picture any way they wish. Fantasy and imagination have free rein. However, the more specific kinetic instructions (asking that the people in drawings be doing something and the drawer include himself in the picture) produce drawings from which it is much easier to discern the child's perception of himself relative to others. The inclusion of movement in drawings enriches or adds to the data available to the interpreter.

84

For Both Akinetic and Kinetic Drawings

The child is given a sheet of 8½"x11" paper and a medium soft pencil, and asked to draw the group and kind of drawing you have chosen. If he asks for more specific instructions or some kind of direction, repeat the original instructions or make some nondirective remark. When obtaining drawings from groups of children, seat them as far apart as possible to minimize copying. If the child does not name the members of the group in his drawing or identify them in some way, then ask him to do this when the picture is finished.

For Akinetic Drawings

  Draw-a-Family (DAF) Technique

"I'd like you to draw your family."

  Draw-a-Classroom (DAC) Technique

This instruction comes from Kutnick (1978): "Draw me a picture of a classroom with people in it."

For Kinetic Drawings

  Draw-a-Group (DAG) Technique

The instructions which follow are taken from Hare and Hare (1956):

> "Think of the children you like to play with most on the playground. Now think of the things you like to do best with this group of children. Then draw a picture of your group doing the thing you like best. When you are through, we will write down what is going on in your picture."

  Kinetic Family Drawing (KFD) Technique

The following instructions are taken from Burns and Kaufman (1970):

> "Draw a picture of everyone in your family, including you, doing something. Try to draw whole people, not cartoons or stick figures. Remember, make everyone doing something, some kind of action."

85

Kinetic School Drawing (KSD) Technique

The instructions below are taken from Prout and Phillips (1974):

> "I'd like you to draw a school picture. Put yourself, your teacher and a friend or two in the picture. Make everyone doing something. Try to draw whole people and make the best drawing you can. Remember, draw yourself, your teacher and a friend or two, and make everyone doing something."

The instructions spelled out here are for the more commonly used group drawing techniques. Actually, the types of groups which could be used are unlimited. Depending on the purpose, you could give either kinetic or akinetic instructions to obtain drawings of groups such as church, club, baseball or other sports teams, Girl Scouts or Boy Scouts, 4-H and many others.

INTERPRETATION OF GROUP DRAWINGS

Overall Impression

Obtaining the overall impression or main message from *akinetic* group drawings may be difficult. It is much easier in the case of *kinetic* drawings, which are projectively richer. Ask yourself questions like, "Are the members of the group all engaged in the same or similar activities? Are they doing something different? Is there total interaction, interaction between only a few, or completely independent functioning? The answers will tell you whether a family or group is cohesive or not cohesive, constructive or destructive, happy or unhappy.

Specific Indicators or Signs

1. Omission of Figures: Who is left out of a child's drawing? It is important to know. Omission of the self suggests a poor self-concept, feelings of being left out and feelings of insignificance. In family drawings, it is significant if a family member is left out; omissions may indicate concern or poor feelings about or rejection of that person. In school drawings, it is significant if the teacher is omitted. This may represent a negative attitude toward school or teacher.

2. Inclusion of Extra Figures: Extra figures included in drawings should be noted. In family drawings, siblings, grandparents, aunts, uncles, and other relatives may be added. Pets are often found in drawings. Children include significant people in their drawings. In some cases, the extra person is a friend, or the drawer may wish the person to be his friend.

3. Placement of Figures on the Page: Distance is an important variable in the interpretation of group drawings. Children may place themselves next to the parent, teacher, sibling, or another individual because they like that person. However, sometimes children who wish to be closer to or want more attention from a person will draw themselves next to that person. Those who view themselves as left out or not part of a group will often draw themselves apart from others. Similarly, those who wish to be away from a certain person may draw themselves at some distance from that person.

Overprotected children or those desiring attention may place themselves between their parents. If there are several children and little rivalry between them, a child may draw all family members in chronological order with the size of the figures corresponding to their age.

4. Relative Size of Figures: The size of those included in the drawing is important. If a child perceives another classmate or sibling as being more important, he may draw him larger than himself, even though in real life the drawer is larger. Children who view themselves as insignificant relative to others draw themselves tiny. Sometimes aggressive adults or even other children are drawn large. A word of caution: Individuals in group drawings are often drawn smaller and in less detail than those produced for DAP drawings. One must be careful, therefore, not to interpret them in exactly the same way as individual "person" drawings.

5. Similar Treatment of Figures: A child may draw himself to look like someone he admires or is fond of. He may draw himself facing the same direction or wearing similar clothing or in some other way identify himself with the favored person.

6. Differential Treatment of Figures: If there is rivalry between family members, the individual may be drawn differently, i.e., unhappy face, uncomplimentary pose.

7. Underlining or Baselining: Children who perceive their families as insecure may draw a line under the family members. Underlining represents structure and provides a secure base. Some children may draw the family at the bottom of the page, using the edge for a secure baseline. Children who feel insecure in the classroom may also use underlining and baselining.

8. Separation of Individual by Lines or Encapsulation: Unwanted family members are often separated from others by lines or by being boxed off. If a family does not often "do things together," each member may be compartmentalized and each engaged in a different activity. In the classroom, if the child views himself as isolated, he may draw a box or circle around himself.

9. If two individuals are *engaged in the same activity,* there may be rivalry between them. This is especially true for those drawn taking part in ballgames, hockey, spelling bees, and the like.

10. There are many *actions* in kinetic drawings which take on significance. You may wish to refer to Burns and Kaufman (1970, 1972) and Burns (1982) for a detailed interpretation of KFDs. These authors view a mother cooking as one who is nurturing, and a mother ironing as one who is trying to give warmth. Cleaning mothers have been described as being more oriented to things than to people. Fathers playing with their children or paying bills are considered to be normal. Those who are portrayed driving may be away from home so much that the children miss them. Fathers drawn cutting the lawn or chopping wood are seen as tough.

Examples of Drawings
Measuring
Self in Relation to Others

DRAWING 1: "I feel left out."

The Drawer
    Yvonne, age six; adopted, doing poorly at school

The Projection
    Overall Impression: Some family interaction; self feels left out
    Specific Indicators:
      • Placement of self at end of page, though not youngest (feels less important or wanted than the others, even the dog, which is drawn ahead of herself)

• No hair on self (perceives herself as "different" from the others)
• Baselining (perceives family as insecure)
• Partial encapsulation of herself and possibly mother (unwanted family members are often separated by lines or by being boxed off)
• Written phrase "Hi Yvonne" (expresses a wish to be close to Dad)
• Light (indicates need for warmth and affection)

90

DRAWING 2: "I want Mom to love me."

The Drawer
Donald, age eight; poor student; very
unhappy at school; rejected by mother.

The Projection
Overall Impression: Very unhappy
Specific Indicators:
- Mother only person drawn; father very
  faint and tiny (mother, or the lack of
  her, is the most important factor in his
  life)
- Mother making breakfast (she is perceived as nurturing)
- All children are pictured sleeping
  (sometimes suggests depression or
  unhappiness)
- Donald drawn close to mother (he
  wants her love and approval)

DRAWING 3: "I miss my dad."

The Drawer
> Carl, age nine, above-average intelligence, depressed in school; school personnel do not know reason for his unhappiness.

The Projection
> *Overall Impression:* Family lacking in cohesion
>
> *Specific Indicators:*
> - Compartmentalization (if a family does not often "do things together," each member may be boxed off and each drawn doing something different)
> - Mother drawn ironing (she is perceived as nurturing)
> - Father drawn driving a truck (he is often away from home)

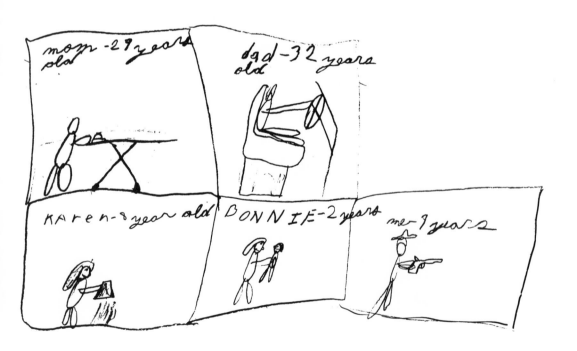

DRAWING 4: "Nobody cares about me."

The Drawer
   Bill, age 10, slow learner with severe reading problems, unhappy in school, mother a former psychiatric patient.

The Projection
   Overall Impression: Feeling of isolation
   Specific Indicators:
   • Self separated from rest of family and with back view (feelings of isolation and rejection)
   • Other family members engaged in similar activities (compounding the isolation)
   • Watching TV (does he relate better to objects than to people?)

DRAWING 5: "You're my hero, Dad."

The Drawer
    Sean, age eight, doing well in school, iden-
    tifies with father, some rivalry between him
    and his sister.

The Projection
    Overall Impression: Cohesive family with
    normal sibling rivalry.
    Specific Indicators:
        • Placement of self next to father (likes to
          be close with his father)
        • Father's name in double lettering (again
          indicating his importance in Sean's
          eyes)
        • Sister drawn with frown and placed be-
          tween parents; sister is drawn differ-
          ently, indicating some sibling rivalry

DRAWING 6: "My brother bugs me."

The Drawer
Tanya, age six, sister to Sean (see drawing #5) no problems at school, sibling rivalry, identifies with mother.

The Projection
Overall Impression: Normal identification with parent of the same sex.
Specific Indicators:
- Placement next to mother (identifies particulary with mother; note that the house separates them from father and brother)
- Brother drawn largest of all (perceived as significant and as a rival)

DRAWING 7: "I wish my Dad was well again."

The Drawer
Glori, age seven, above-average ability; behavior problem in home and school; father recently had heart attack; closer to mother.

The Projection
Overall Impression: Family fairly cohesive; dad is viewed differently.
Specific Indicators:
- Placement near mother (identifies more with mother)
- Mother watering (perceived as nurturing)
- Father drawn without legs and on baseline (may indicate insecurity resulting from heart attack)
- Father cutting grass (fathers drawn cutting the grass are seen as tough. . .in this case, could be a wish to have him restored to former strength)
- House and walk separate mother and Glori from father, sister and brother

98

DRAWING 8: "I'm scared of my Dad."

The Drawer
Larry, age nine, difficulty relating to others, poor relationship with father

The Projection
Overall Impression: Family lacking in cohesiveness.
Specific Indicators:
- Father drawn large (father perceived as aggressive)
- Father cutting grass (fathers drawn cutting grass are seen as tough)
- Compartmentalization (family members separated and engaged in different activities)

me

Hayley, 9

Connie, 12

mom

Dad

100

DRAWING 9: "Why me?"

The Drawer

Nick, age nine, doing well in school, middle child, stable family relationships, perceives himself as having to do more chores than others.

The Projection

Overall Impression: Family perceived as lacking cohesion.

Specific Indicators:
- Compartmentalization (family does not often "do things together")
- Mother vacuuming (a cleaning mother is regarded as being more oriented to things than to people)

- Frown on Nick's face (resents having to put the dishes away)
- Father drawn cutting grass (usually means father is perceived as tough)

N.B. This drawing and the next two (#10 and #11) show how children in the same family can perceive their family differently.

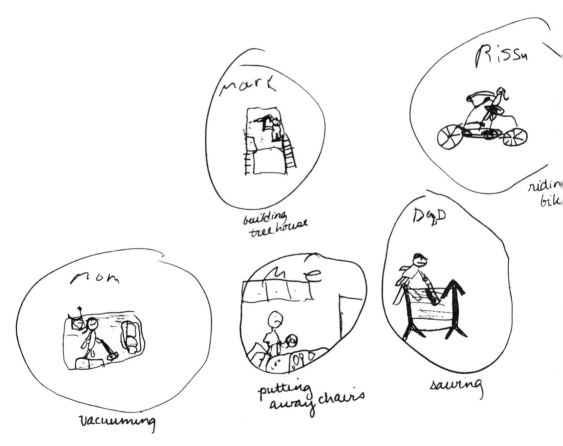

DRAWING 10: "I want Mom and Dad to
like me best."

The Drawer
Mark, brother of Nick (see drawing #9), age
11, sensitive, oldest in family.

The Projection
Overall Impression: Happy family.
Specific Indicators:
- Self drawn close to parents (he likes to
  be near those he loves)
- A box separates other family members
  from himself and parents (does not
  want them to come between him and
  his parents)
- Loving interaction between parents (he
  is very sensitive to people's feelings
  about each other)

Nick

Rissa
opening
present

Mark

Mom and
Dad

Today
I am going
to fix my

DRAWING 11: "Off I go on my horse."

The Drawer
Rissa, age seven, sister of Nick and Mark (see drawings #9 and #10) doing well in school, youngest in family.

The Projection
Overall Impression: Family perceived as lacking cohesion; individual activities perceived as more important than group activities.
Specific Indicators:
- Compartmentalization (family members drawn engaged in different activities)
- Mother cleaning (usually indicates a person more oriented to things than to people)
- Self-emphasis ("Me" is drawn higher than anyone else, i.e., on a horse)

DRAWING 12: "Everyone likes Harold."

The Drawer
   Jim, age 10, low-average ability, doing poorly in school, oldest in family, very jealous of next brother Harold; mother extremely capable and the dominant member of the family.

The Projection
   Overall Impression: Dominance of brother Harold
   Specific Indicators:
      • Brother placed at top of page (he is the "favored" one and the only one working)
      • Self at bottom (feels inferior)
      • Mother largest figure and only one with hands (she is the most capable)
      • Father drawn small (he is insignificant in comparison)

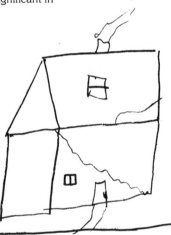

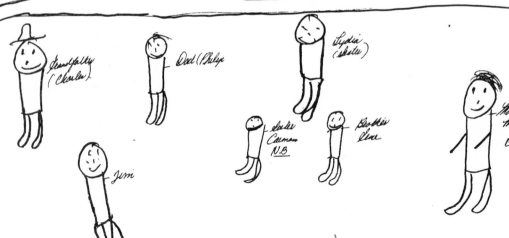

DRAWING 13: "I want Mom to love me."

The Drawer

Cameron, age seven, learning problems, social and emotional problems in both home and school. Did not bond with mother in critical early years; younger brother favored by mother, who dislikes Cameron; father indifferent to him.

The Projection

Overall Impression: Disturbed family relationship

Specific Indicators:

- Placement of favored sibling next to mother
- Breast and belly button emphases (very unusual figure treatment, probably indicating unmet attachment needs)

105

DRAWING 14: Kinetic School Drawing:
"I don't think she likes me."

The Drawer
Dan, age six, with poor self-concept

The Projection
Overall Impression: Uncertainty
Specific Indicators:
- Frown on teacher's face (not a happy person)
- No features on own face (poor self-concept)
- Writing on drawing (suggests mixed feelings about school and teacher)

DRAWING 15: "I'm pretty important, you know."

The Drawer
Bree, age six and a half, above-average intelligence, has brother age four, tends to think she is "hard done by" when punished or made to work.

The Projection
Overall Impression: Happy, healthy family drawing, members "do things together"
Specific Indicators:
- Mother and brother picking carrots, father digging, self watering (all nurturing activities)
- Placement next to father who is facing in her direction (likes to have his approval)
- Subject is largest figure, dressed differently from mom, doing the most pleasant job (aware of her own importance)
- Line separates self from family (further emphasizes her importance)

DRAWING 16: Kinetic School Drawing:
"I need to have friends."

The Drawer
　　Laurie, age eight and a half, average ability,
　　Cree Indian child living with foster parents
　　because of very unstable home environ-
　　ment, severe language disability, and mark-
　　ed problems with social relationships

The Projection
　　Overall Impression: Self different from
　　others
　　Specific Indicators:
　　　　• Self is circled (she perceives herself as
　　　　　different and feels isolated)
　　　　• Written phrase ("my friend" is repeated
　　　　　many times, indicating a desperate
　　　　　need to have friends)
　　　　• Shading on feet (anxiety about herself)
　　　　• Shading on non-friends' faces (anxiety
　　　　　about people other than her friends,
　　　　　whose faces in the drawing are un-
　　　　　shaded)

DRAWING 17: "Hey, look at me and MY
                        FISH!"

The Drawer
    Bree, age seven, above-average intelli-
    gence, has younger brother, likes the lime-
    light (see drawing #15)

The Projection
    Overall Impression: A happy, healthy fam-
    ily drawing
    Specific Indicators:
        • All family members engaged in same
          activity (often "do things together")
        • Self is largest figure making the largest
          catch (has strong self-concept)

DRAWING 18: "Sometimes I wish I were
a baby again."

The Drawer
Scott, age four, very bright, has baby sister
10 months, some normal sibling rivalry,
which often becomes more evident when
the baby reaches the crawling and walking
stages.

The Projection
Overall Impression: Unhappy, except for
baby
Specific Indicators:
- Encapsulation (self and baby sister are
  circled and centered, indicating importance of what is happening between
  them)
- Placement of self in buggy (a wish to remain a baby and command more attention)
- Smile on baby (she enjoys pulling his
  hair!)
- Omission of body and arms on self
  (feels helpless because he is not allowed
  to retaliate)
- Frowns (indicating unhappiness over
  situation)

CHAPTER 6

DRAWINGS AS A MEASURE
OF GROUP VALUES

RESEARCH TO DATE

It was Dennis (1966) who first advocated the use of drawings as a measure of group social values. He considered this the third major use of HFDs, the first being their use as a measure of development by Goodenough (1926), and the second their use as a measure of personality by Machover (1949). Unlike his predecessors, Dennis focused on the *content* of the drawings. He was not interested in their size, the pressure on the pencil, erasures or firmness of line. He was interested in the *kind* of men drawn; that is, whether they were soldiers or farmers, bankers or beggars, and so on. He believed that children generally draw men they admire and who are thought of favorably by their societies. If this were true, children's drawings would reveal the values of their respective groups insofar as they can be represented visually.

Dennis, who incidentally confined his research to boys, considered the following features in drawings to be negative: old people, spectacles, crossed eyes, facial scars, mouth drawn down, tattoos, crippled men, fat men, patched clothing, and an eyepatch. When analyzing drawings, he looked at factors such as modern versus traditional dress, emphasis on masculinity, facial expression, religious content, the representation of work or a job, the diversity of social roles, physical features like hair style, and the presence of ridicule and humor.

Although the placement of HFDs on the page is often attributed to personality factors, Dennis felt it could be influenced by culture as well. Since culture determines the position on a page at which a person begins to write, he maintained that this will affect the placement of a person's drawing. In a 1958 study, he compared the drawings of Americans and Armenians, whose writing starts on the upper-left of a page, with a group of Lebanese and Egyptians, who begin on the upper-right side. While the subject's drawings were more frequently found in the quadrant of the page within which he began to write, the relationship between drawing placement and culture was unclear. He therefore urged caution in the interpretation of cross-cultural differences in the location of drawings on a page. In 1960, Dennis along with Raskin, compared top-left handwriting groups (Turks, Cambodians, Japanese) with the top-right handwriting (Iranians, Israelis). This time his findings were more supportive of the "motor transfer hypothesis." The five linguistic groups located their drawings in the quadrant of the page within which writing begins to a greater degree than in any other quadrant. He emphasized that a factor other than personality plays a marked role in creating group differences in the location of drawings.

Measure of Cultural Values

Using over 2500 drawings from different parts of the world and from different groups within the U.S.A., Dennis found differences in cultural values. Within the U.S.A., the drawings of Christians, Jews, blacks, and Navajos were fairly similar and Dennis concluded that the American culture manages to achieve a uniform set of values. Nearly all the drawings of blacks represented white men! European drawings were different from those by Americans, in that they were high in masculinity and diversity scores and moderate in smiling.

Anastasi and Foley (1936) also found differences in content when they examined the spontaneous drawings of children from different cultures. The drawings were part of an international exhibition of children's paintings from 41 countries. Political activities were especially prominent in the drawings from Spain and Russia. War or fighting was illustrated in drawings from Bali, China, Greece, Italy, Spain, and Yugoslavia. Religious content was featured in the drawings from Canada, Ireland, Finland, Germany, Palestine, Scotland, Sweden, and Switzerland.

For his study of Thai children's drawings, Gardiner (1974) required his subjects to draw both a man and a woman. The children depicted significantly more people in modern than in traditional dress. Oriental features were highly characteristic of the 500 drawings. The drawings of women contained significantly more religious content than the drawings of men. Sixty-eight percent of the drawings depicted smiling faces. None drew a person working or being gainfully employed.

The HFDs of Navajo kindergarten children were studied by Thurber (1976). Since earlier studies had indicated that the boys drew better than girls because of the high value placed on artistic achievement, the present study was undertaken to find out if artistic achievement was still highly valued. The drawings were scored according to Goodenough-Harris criteria, in which detail and proportion are considered. No significant differences were found between males and females. Thurber suggested that the detachment of these children from traditional values may have lessened the different artistic stimulation for boys and girls.

The cultural values of Canadian Cree Indian children, grades kindergarten through grade nine were the subject of an unpublished study by Klepsch (1981). The children reside on a reservation and attend school on the reservation. The school is new with all modern conveniences and amenities. Every attempt is made to emphasize the Cree Indian culture in the curriculum and to incorporate it into subject matter. The teachers are white, with the exception of the principal, who is Metis (half Indian, half white). Teacher aides and other school employees are native.

In this study, 122 drawings were obtained, a sampling of which are to be found at the end of this chapter. These were examined for a number of specific indicators, with the following results:

For Smiling vs. Non-smiling Faces: Eighty percent of the children drew smiling faces, while only 20 percent drew non-smiling faces. Most of the non-smiling faces came from older children, particularly from those in grades five, six, eight, and nine. In fact, in grades eight and nine, there were more non-smiling faces than smiling.

For Clothing (Traditional vs. Modern): Fourteen percent of the children drew a person in traditional clothing, while 41 percent drew their person in modern attire. It was impossible to differentiate the clothing in 45 percent of the drawings.

For Hair Style (Traditional vs. Modern): Twenty percent of the hair styles were judged as traditional and 41 percent as modern. It was impossible to score 39 percent of the drawings as to type of hair style.

For Symbols (Traditional vs. Modern, Religious): Traditional symbols (arrows, spears, etc.) were found in 8 percent of the drawings, and modern symbols (cars, TV sets, etc.) in 16 percent. Religious symbols were discerned in only two drawings, one from a third grader, another from an eighth grader.

For Masculinity or Femininity Emphasis: Many drawings were very feminine or masculine in appearance. Forty-one percent of the children emphasized their sexuality, while 59 percent did not.

For People Drawn Working: Only seven drawings were of people working, most of them students in class.

For Ridicule and Humor: Eleven percent of the children (mostly from grades five, six, and seven) depicted this kind of cynicism in their drawings.

For Hostility and Aggression: Only four drawings contained these variables.

A component of this study was a comparison of the drawings of third grade Cree children with drawings of third graders from a white school. The Indian drawings contained more traditional hair styles and clothing than did the drawings of whites. While not one white drawing portrayed work, one Indian child drew a person working. Smiles were present in 93 percent of the Indian drawings, while 73 percent of the whites drew a person smiling.

The Klepsch study produced three findings of interest:

1. Indian children typically drew more white-looking persons than Indian-looking persons. Between 14 and 20 percent of the drawings were judged to contain Indian features (no drawings done by white children were of Indians or of any other person from a different culture).
2. Among the third graders, more Indians drew themselves smiling than whites.
3. Older Indian children represented more cynicism, ridicule and humor in their drawings than younger children.

Measure of Religious Values

Dennis found little or no religious content in the drawings of most culturally different groups. To find out if those who placed a high value on religion did, in fact, include religious content in their drawings Dennis, along with Uras (1965), examined 100 drawings made by nuns. Religious content was found in 74 percent of the drawings and supported the authors' thesis that strong religious values will be reflected in drawings. The most numerous religious symbols found were crosses and the most common central figures were saints, angels, priests, monks, and Christ.

Measure of Hostility

Gardiner (1969) studied over 2000 drawings of boys ages 10 through 13, from 26 cultural groups, to measure and compare variations in the occurrence of hostility. He found evidence of hostility in 35 percent of the drawings from Thailand, followed by Germany with 26 percent, Taiwan with 25 percent, Algeria with 15 percent, Iran with 3 percent and Japan with 1 percent. (One could speculate that the scores might have been different in the 1980s, at least for the Iranians!) Among the most notable variations in hostile content was the emphasis upon cowboys and men in modern dress with guns in Thai drawings, ancient European and American Indian warriors in those from Germany, and figures of modern soldiers in the drawings from Taipei.

Measure of Cooperation

In a study to determine children's expressions of cooperation and other values and attitudes, Smart and Smart (1975) compared the drawings of 11- and 12-year-old boys and girls in Australia, Canada, England, New Zealand, and the United States. A variation of Dennis' (1966) Draw-a-Man task was administered; the subjects were asked to draw the self plus another person doing something. The researchers found that U.S. boys and girls drew more smiling faces than did any other group. This was consistent with Dennis' previous findings. Dyad scores showed U.S. children to be high in smiling and low in competition, games and sports, and work. New Zealand and Canadian scores showed many similarities, being high in cooperation and work. English children ranked highest in competition and Australian children in humor. The most striking difference between the American drawings and all the others was in the small amount of content indicating action and involvement with other people!

Measure of Racial Identity

Schofield (1978) tested another modification of Dennis' approach (in which crayons instead of pencils were used) to get a measure of racial identity. Black and white children were given the drawing task to find out if black children were accepting of their racial identity. In scoring, factors such as color of the face and skin, as well as hairstyle and color, were examined. Findings indicated that whites were more likely to draw figures that were clearly white than blacks were to draw figures that were clearly black. White children were less likely to draw blacks than blacks were to draw whites. Black children were more likely to avoid giving a clear indication of race in the figure they drew than were whites. Kuhlman, who replicated Schofield's study in 1979, found similar results, suggesting blacks to be less accepting of their racial identity than whites. Surprisingly, all these conclusions were similar to those reached by Dennis in 1966. However, Coyle and Eisenman (1970) have suggested that children's use of color may have nothing at all to do with racial identification. It could reflect a learning history. In their study, black and white children were asked to fill in with crayons an outline of a Santa Claus face. As expected, both black and white children tended to depict Santa as a white man. However, in spite of giving him Caucasian features, black children often colored the beard with skin tones of brown and black as well as white. The white children, on the other hand, used white and red for the beard and generally preferred brighter colors. Indeed, color may be culturally determined. Anastasi and Foley (1936) found distinct differences in its use. Brilliant and frequently gaudy colors were used in the drawings of American Indians and of children from Bali, Chile, Colombia, Costa Rica, Czechoslovakia, France, Germany, Hawaii, Hungary, Lithuania, Mexico, and Tunisia. Light pastels were favored in the drawings from China, Denmark, Greece, Ireland, Italy, Jamaica, Turkey, and Yugoslavia. Darker colors were often seen in drawings from England, Japan, Scotland, and the U.S.S.R.

Measure of Racial Difference

Bromberg and Hutchinson (1974) compared the drawings of Indian and white individuals and found a most striking difference in the treatment of the eyes. The Indians' eyes were open, alert and almost glaring in quality, and it was felt that this was because Indians used their eyes to comprehend the environment and pick up clues about the behavior and attitude of others. In spite of changed lifestyles, this ability to observe may still be a characteristic to a certain extent of some persons of native ancestry. Klepsch thinks this could well explain why he obtained more detailed, lifelike drawings of superior quality from the Cree Indian children in his study on cultural values than he usually does from white children.

Several studies have examined the sex of the drawing made by subjects when instructed to draw a person. Burton (1972) compared the drawings of Barbados children from intact and fatherless homes, respectively. In fatherless homes, there was a greater likelihood for the drawing to be female than in the intact homes. In both fatherless and intact groups, 76 percent of the boys drew a man, while 82 percent of the girls drew a woman. Burton compared his results with figures from the U.S., in which 85 percent of the boys drew a man and only 65 percent of the girls drew a woman. He attributed the greater number of female drawings in both boys and girls from the Barbados to the matrifocal family in the Caribbean culture, in which the female controls most of the resources.

Male and female Jordanian university students were given the Draw-a-Person task by Daoud (1976). Of the male subjects, 82 percent drew the male figure, while only 52 percent of the female subjects drew a female figure. The differences in these drawings were attributed to the fact that the Jordanian culture is male-dominated.

A comparison of the sex of the person drawn by Japanese, Navajo, and American white and black seven-year-olds was made by Henderson, Butler, Goffeney, Saito and Clarkson (1971). When the sexes were pooled across the four races, a highly significant difference was found between the sexes in the proportion of self-sex figures drawn. Girls drew their self-sex more frequently than boys, but both sexes drew their own sex more frequently than the opposite. The tendency to draw self-sex was strongest among the Japanese.

In the Mexican culture, Laosa, Swartz and Diaz-Guerrero (1974) found that girls, in later childhood and early adolescence, drew males more often than females when the DAP task was given. The investigators felt this was due to the values in the Mexican culture, in which girls live relatively sheltered lives, are expected to defer to others, and avoid the appearance of superior intellectual ambitions. In males, manliness and "machismo" are stressed.

A comparison of the drawings of American and Filipino children was undertaken by Rabin and Limuaco (1959). At the time of this study, the American culture was viewed as overlapping in sex roles, while in the Filipino culture sex roles were considered distinct and more akin to those of earlier American times. In order to discover the clarity and intensity of sexual differentiation in the two cultures, children were asked for two drawings, one of a person and the other of a person of the opposite sex. Filipino children were significantly better than Americans at providing a clear-cut indication of the sex of their drawing. The authors concluded that this was due to the clear-cut sex roles in the Filipino culture.

Again, in a study to assess the relative social dominance of males versus females, Patalano (1977) instructed 30 black and 30 white male drug abusers to draw both a person and a person of the other sex. The mean height and area of the female figures drawn by black subjects were greater than for the white subjects. Patalano suggested that female dominance may be related to cultural and familial upbringing, since there were many fatherless family constellations in the black population.

INSTRUCTIONS FOR ADMINISTRATION

The instructions for obtaining drawings to measure group values are slightly different from those for obtaining drawings to measure personality. Give the child a piece of 8½"x11" paper and a medium soft pencil. Then simply say,

"I'd like you to draw a picture of a whole person."

If a child asks for more specific instructions or some kind of direction, repeat the original instructions or make a non-directive type of remark indicating that any kind of person may be drawn.

For a child who is very young or does not understand what the word *person* means, the instructions should be repeated as follows:

"I'd like you to draw a picture of a whole person. You can draw any kind of person you want – a man, or a woman, or a girl or a boy."

When groups of children are asked to draw, care should be taken to seat the children as far apart as possible to minimize copying.

INTERPRETATION OF DRAWINGS

Specific Indicators or Signs

(Numbers 1 to 8 in this section have been adapted from Dennis' work (1966).)

1. *The type of clothing,* traditional or modern, gives us a clue as to whether the group or individual producing the drawing(s) values the traditional or the contemporary. An indication of clothing, costume or

style characteristic of former societies suggests that the past is valued. More modern attire and style of the day suggest that the present is valued more than the past.

2. *Facial characteristics and hairstyle* characteristic of different races give clues to racial identity. Features which characterize certain races include curly hair, braided hair, shape of eyes, form of nose and mouth. Again, individuals and groups who value their race will tend to draw themselves with these distinctive features. Those who do not will deemphasize the features and perhaps draw more Caucasian-looking individuals.

3. *Masculinity* or *femininity* will be emphasized by those who view this as important. Masculine drawings will often feature facial hair, beards, moustaches and long hair. The figure will be muscular or dressed in the masculine attire of soldiers, policemen, and athletes. Feminine-looking figures will have feminine-looking hair which will be drawn well-groomed. Clothing will be feminine, and probably dresses will be worn. Attention will be given to details such as eyelashes, jewelry and fingernails.

4. *Smiling or non-smiling faces.* Smiling faces suggest cooperation, while non-smiling faces suggest a lack of cooperation. Both corners of the mouth must turn upward before an individual is considered smiling.

5. Individuals drawn *working* suggest that work is valued. The kind of work he or she is drawn doing suggests the specific types of work that are valued.

6. The incluson of *religious symbols* in drawings suggests religious values. These symbols include crosses, rosary beads, Christ-like figures, religious people, i.e. nuns, priests, ministers, monks, rabbis.

7. *Ridicule* and *humor* in drawings suggest sarcasm and a cynical view of life. They may also be drawn by hostile individuals who are suspicious and reluctant to reveal themselves.

8. A drawing of a person in a *social role* suggests the types of roles that are most valued by a given group. Examples are drawings of teachers, farmers, cowboys, students, policemen, politicians, etc.

9. *Hostility* and *aggression* are suggested when soldiers, people with weapons, or individuals in combat are drawn. Aggressive figures tend to be drawn rather large.

10. *Racial color* is portrayed by those who value it. In pencil drawings, black, representing the negroid race, can readily be portrayed. However, crayons may be a better medium for representing color, particularly if individuals of different skin color are among the drawers.

11. The *sex* of the person drawn indicates which sex is more valued within a given group. If females draw a man when asked to draw a person, then probably men are more valued than women. On the other hand, if boys draw a woman when asked to draw a person, then it is likely women are highly valued.

12. *Symbols* in drawings often indicate whether traditional or modern culture is the more valued. Traditional symbols include drums, arrows, horses, headdresses, spears, tents and beadwork, while modern symbols are TV sets, cars, motorcycles, snowmobiles, light bulbs, radio antennae, modern-looking houses and other items characteristic of contemporary living.

Examples of Drawings
Measuring
Group Values

DRAWING 1

The Drawer
   Sixth grade Cree Indian girl

The Projection
   Overall Impression: Traditional
   Specific Indicators:
   - Clothing (traditional, past is valued)
   - Hairstyle (traditional, past is valued)
   - Posture (traditional, past is valued)
   - Smile (cooperative)

DRAWING 2

The Drawer
   Fifth grade Cree Indian boy

The Projection
   Overall Impression: Ridicule
   Specific Indicator:
      • Ridicule and humor (suggest sarcasm
        and a cynical view of life; may also be
        drawn by suspicious individuals who
        are reluctant to reveal themselves)

DRAWING 3

The Drawer
    Fifth grade Cree Indian girl

The Projection
    Overall Impression: Traditional
    Specific Indicators:
        • Hairstyle (traditional, past valued)
        • Smile (cooperative)
        • Heart symbol (loving)

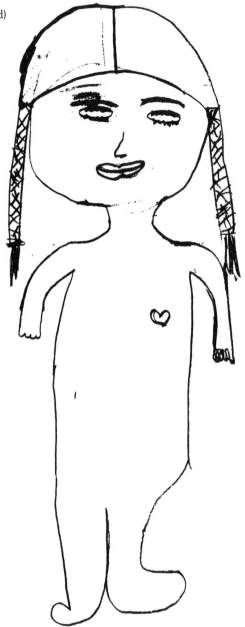

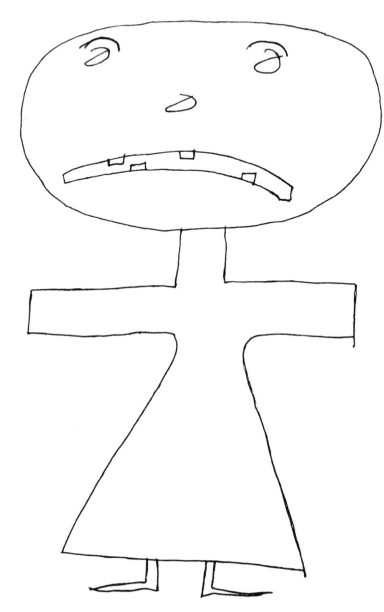

DRAWING 4

The Drawer
Eighth grade Cree Indian girl

The Projection
   Overall Impression: Hostility
   Specific Indicators:
      • Ridicule and humor (suggest sarcasm
        and cynical view of life; may also be
        drawn by hostile individuals who are
        reluctant to reveal themselves)
      • Unsmiling mouth with teeth (hostile)

DRAWING 5

The Drawer
    Second grade Cree Indian girl

The Projection
    Overall Impression: Traditional
    Specific Indicators:
        • Smile (cooperative)
        • Hairstyle (traditional, values past)
        • Beadwork (symbol valuing past)
        • Eyelashes, beads, earrings (femininity important)

126

DRAWING 6

The Drawer
    Fifth grade Cree Indian boy

The Projection
    Overall Impression: Traditional
    Specific Indicators:
        • Horse (traditional symbol)
        • Clothing, riding (masculinity)
        • Gun (hostility)

DRAWING 7

The Drawer
    Sixth grade Cree Indian girl

The Projection
    Overall Impression: Traditional
    Specific Indicators:
- Clothing (traditional, past is valued)
- Spear (people with weapons suggest hostility and aggression)
- Headdress (traditional symbol)
- Drew person of opposite sex (males are important)

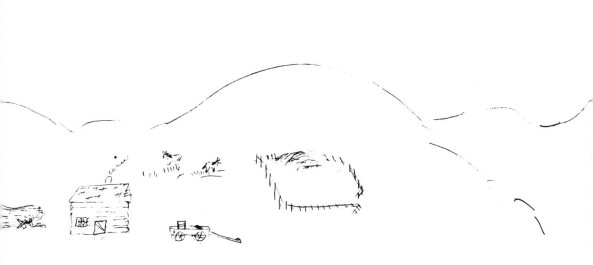

DRAWING 8

The Drawer
  Fifth grade Cree Indian boy

The Projection
  Overall Impression: Traditional
  Specific Indicators:
    • Scene depicts life and work on reservation (values past)
    • No person depicted (objects and animals valued more than people?)

DRAWING 9

The Drawer
    Seventh grade Cree Indian girl

The Projection
    Overall Impression: Modern
    Specific Indicators:
        • Modern home, garage, car, electric
        lights (symbols valuing present)
        • Objects emphasized more than people

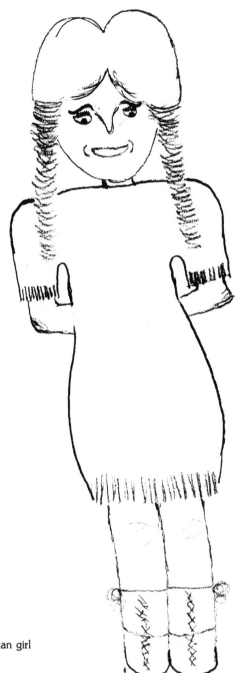

DRAWING 10

The Drawer
    Eighth grade Cree Indian girl

The Projection
    Overall Impression: Traditional
    Specific Indicators:
        • Type of clothing (traditional, valuing
          past)
        • Type of hairstyle (traditional, valuing
          past)
        • Smile (cooperative)

132

DRAWING 11

The Drawer
    Third grade Cree Indian boy

The Projection
    Overall Impression: Modern
    Specific Indicators:
        • Modern home, TV antenna, car, radio
          antenna (all symbols valuing present)
        • Smile (cooperative)

133

DRAWING 12

The Drawer
   Sixth grade Cree Indian girl

The Projection
   Overall Impression: Modern
   Specific Indicators:
      • Hairstyle (modern)
      • Dress (modern)
      • Accessories (stressing femininity)

DRAWING 13

The Drawer
Seventh grade Cree Indian boy

The Projection
Overall Impression: Ridicule and humor
Specific Indicators:
- Ridicule and humor (suggest sarcasm and a cynical view of life; may be drawn by hostile individuals who are suspicious and reluctant to reveal themselves)
- Hair, moustache and broad shoulders (masculinity is important)

DRAWING 14

The Drawer
   Fifth grade Cree Indian boy

The Projection
   Overall Impression: Modern
   Specific Indicators:
      • Figure is boxing (an activity suggesting
        aggression and masculinity)

DRAWING 15

The Drawer
Sixth grade Cree Indian boy

The Projection
Overall Impression: Ridicule and humor
Specific Indicators:
- Ridicule and humor (suggest sarcasm and a cynical view of life; may be drawn by hostile individuals who are suspicious and reluctant to reveal themselves)

DRAWING 16

The Drawer
Eighth grade Cree Indian boy

The Projection
Overall Impression: Ridicule and humor
Specific Indicators:
- Ridicule and humor (suggest sarcasm and a cynical view of life; may be drawn by hostile individuals who are suspicious and reluctant to reveal themselves)
- Teeth (hostility)

DRAWING 17

The Drawer
Fifth grade Cree Indian boy

The Projection
Overall Impression: Modern, strength
Specific Indicators:
- Weight-lifting (modern activity demonstrating strength)
- Hair, strong arms (masculinity valued)

DRAWING 18

The Drawer
   Eighth grade Cree Indian boy

The Projection
   Overall Impression: Ridicule and humor
   Specific Indicators:
      • Ridicule and humor (suggests sarcasm
        and a cynical view of life; may be drawn
        by hostile individuals who are suspici-
        ous and reluctant to reveal themselves)
      • Moustache, goatee, hair (masculinity is
        valued)

140

DRAWING 19

The Drawer
Fourth grade Cree Indian girl

The Projection
Overall Impression: Traditional
Specific Indicators:
- Type of clothing (traditional, past is valued)
- Type of hair style (traditional, past is valued)
- Arrow (traditional symbol)
- Smile (cooperative)

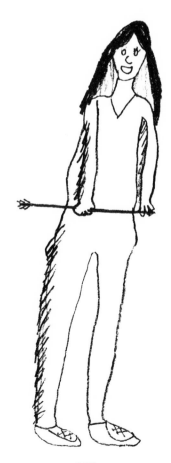

CHAPTER 7

DRAWINGS AS A MEASURE OF ATTITUDES

RESEARCH TO DATE

As early as 1951, in his *Attitudes Handbook,* McMeniman advocated the use of drawings as a measure of attitudes. He was convinced that drawings would add a new dimension to attitude measurement, and that they would give access to a pool of information hitherto untapped by any other measure. He strongly recommended further research into this technique, which he considered full of promise.

However, it was not until some 20 years later that Welch, Flannigan and Rave (1971) used drawings to measure children's attitudes toward their teachers! The study presupposed that children of different ages, with different teachers and attending different schools, project their attitudes towards their teachers in their drawings. Drawings of their teachers were obtained from public and parochial school children in kindergarten through sixth grade. Six patterns emerged from the analysis of the drawings:

1. As early as kindergarten, children tended to identify with an adult of the same sex; boys drew male teachers if they were available, and girls drew female teachers.
2. Boys tended to demonstrate more aggression in their drawings than girls.
3. The amount of aggression for both boys and girls increased as grade level increased.

142

4. As grade level increased, there was more physical structure evident.
5. The drawings of children from parochial schools contained more symbols than those from public schools.
6. Themes such as monsters, robots or Indians occurred repeatedly.

Although the Draw-a-Teacher (DAT) technique was used by Welch et al., it had never been validated. In 1979, Klepsch decided to carry out a validation study. For this particular study, 132 third grade children drew a person and then their teacher. They also responded to the Attitude Toward Teacher and Attitude Toward Learning Process scales of the Arlin-Hills Attitude Surveys (Arlin & Hills, 1976). A weighted scoring system of 13 drawing indicators adapted from a scoring system devised by Engle and Suppes (1970) was used. In a weighted scoring system, each indicator is weighted according to its previously demonstrated predictive power and is not scored as simply being present or absent, e.g., the presence of teeth is scored 4; the omission of hands is scored 2. The following drawing indicators were scored:

> raised arms;
> slanting figure;
> body shading;
> placement on page, i.e. top, bottom, side;
> hair shading;
> head to body ratio (large or small head size);
> humor or theme;
> omission of arms;
> omission of legs;
> presence of teeth;
> erasures;
> size of figure;
> smile.

The drawings of the person and the teacher were each scored using these 13 indicators. An adjusted drawing score was then obtained by comparing the drawings of the teacher and person and scoring only those indicators unique to the drawing of a teacher. If an indicator was present exclusively in the drawing of a teacher, it was assumed that it represented an attitude toward the teacher. Interestingly, only two children drew their person and teacher identically. In the vast majority of the drawings, the teacher was drawn differently from the person. Correlations were calculated:

143

1. between the drawing of a teacher and a person;
2. between the adjusted drawing score and the score from the Attitude Toward Learning Process scale;
3. between the adjusted drawing score and the score from the Attitude Toward Teacher scale; and
4. between the adjusted drawing score and the combined score from the Attitude Toward Learning Process and Attitude Toward Teacher scales.

The correlation between the drawing of a person and the drawing of a teacher was found to be significant. The other correlations proved insignificant.

Since the drawing of a person and a teacher are significantly correlated, it could be argued that it reveals more about the drawer's own personality than about his attitude to the teacher. While a drawer reflects his personality in all that he draws, Klepsch (1980) believes he also reflects an attitude when he draws a specific kind of person. As mentioned before, out of the 132 children who drew both a teacher and a person, only two drew them identically. Presumably, those who drew the teacher differently did so because they were reflecting their attitude in the drawing. Although the correlation between the drawing of a teacher and the drawing of a person was significant, it must be pointed out that it accounted for less than 20 percent of the variance. Therefore, while about 20 percent of what was drawn could be said to relate to personality, over 80 percent of the variance remains unexplained. In Klepsch's view, attitude definitely forms part of this unexplained portion.

The other part of the Klepsch study found no relationship between the drawing scores (projective measure) and scores derived from objective attitude measures (Arlin-Hills Attitude Toward Learning and Attitude Toward Teacher scales). Kahn (1978) and Rimoldi et al. (1975) also found that projective and objective tests do not correlate well. Klepsch feels that drawings dig deeper into the person and assess true attitudes, that is, how the person really views a specific person. These attitudes may be conscious or unconscious. Objective measures, on the other hand, are more likely to reveal the kinds of attitudes the subject perceives the examiner as desiring.

In recent studies, Klepsch has found drawings extremely useful in assessing children's attitudes towards *nurses*, *doctors*, and *dentists*. In the 1980 study, 131 children were asked to draw a picture of their doctor, dentist, and public health nurse. Forty children were in grade one, 48 in grade five and 43 in grade eight. Certain patterns emerged. Nurses were most often drawn with needles. In fact, 25 percent of the

144

drawings of nurses contained them. Since needles are usually viewed as painful, we assumed that their inclusion represented a negative attitude. Dentists were often drawn with very large teeth and/or exaggerated hands and fingers. About 30 percent of the children emphasized these in their drawings. Since dentists work on teeth and use their hands in the process, it may be assumed that large hands and teeth reflect negative attitudes. Several children drew themselves in the dental chair, making the chair very large and themselves very small. It seems as if the children perceive themselves lost or insignificant in the chair. Doctors were drawn wearing glasses much more than any other group, about 30 percent of the time. Since glasses represent learning and knowledge, their inclusion suggests that children view doctors as wise.

In another study (Klepsch, 1975), children's drawings of dental nurses and dentists were compared. One hundred first grade children were asked to draw their dentist and their dental nurse. Dental nurses were drawn with more smiles than dentists. Eighty-seven children drew the dental nurse with a smile, while 75 drew the dentist with a smile. A drill or some other dental instrument appeared more often in the drawings of dentists. Dental instruments were found in 47 percent of the drawings of dentists and in only 20 percent of the drawings of dental nurses. Dental nurses work out of schools and are seen by children quite often. Perhaps they are perceived as smiling, non-threatening persons because they are not always associated with the dental task.

Phillips (1980) assessed the attitudes of a class of second and third grade city children toward health and disease. As part of her study, she asked children to draw a doctor and a nurse. Doctors were usually drawn as male, wearing a stethoscope, head mirror and a smile, while nurses were drawn with a cap with a red cross, and holding a needle!

INSTRUCTIONS FOR ADMINISTRATION

Drawings for measuring attitude are obtained in much the same way as drawings of a person. The difference is that a specific kind of person is requested. Children are provided with a medium soft pencil and a piece of 8½" x 11" paper. Having decided you wish to find out their attitude towards, say, their teacher (or doctor, public health nurse, dentist, policeman, fireman, grocer, priest, minister, etc.), you ask them to draw a picture of that category of person in their life. To obtain the drawing of a teacher then, instruct the children by saying,

"On this piece of paper I would like you to draw a picture of your teacher."

145

If the child asks for specific instructions or some kind of direction, the original instructions should be repeated. If the child draws only part of the person requested, thank him for it and ask him to draw a *whole* teacher. The part of the teacher drawn may be significant since it is this part that comes to his mind when asked to draw.

Never ask the child, "Can you draw a picture of your teacher?" Some children will refuse or deny they are able to draw.

If you ask groups of children to draw, seat the children as far apart as possible to minimize copying, Insecure children lacking confidence will often look to others for their ideas.

INTERPRETATION OF DRAWINGS

Overall Impression

As with the drawings of a person, so with the drawings for measuring attitudes – you should look first at all of the *overall* quality. Ask yourself questions, such as, "Does the kind of person drawn look friendly or unfriendly? Kind or unkind? Gentle or aggressive? Authoritarian or permissive? Likeable or unlikeable? Happy or sad? Ridiculous or sensible?

Specific Indicators or Signs

Next, the drawings should be examined for specific indicators or signs. Some indicators tend to be more associated with negative attitudes, others with positive attitudes. There are still others on which it is hard to pin either a negative or positive value. The list of specific indicators which follows, although by no means exhaustive, has been derived through the scrutiny of hundreds of drawings of teachers, doctors, dentists, public health nurses and dental health nurses.

1. Clown-like figures may be drawn by older children and adolescents to emphasize a point. They often illustrate the "double standard" which youngsters this age are quick to pick up. For example, an overweight doctor or nurse is drawn telling someone to lose weight. A doctor is drawn with a cigarette in his mouth, advising someone to stop smoking; a dentist is drawn with only one tooth, telling someone that daily brushing saves teeth!

2. Drills are frequently seen in drawings of dentists. They are often drawn as rather monster-like creatures, or they are shaded and scribbled over. They are generally associated with pain and discomfort.

146

3. Glasses represent learning and knowledge and stress the intellectual aspects of a person. They are found most often in the drawings of
doctors and teachers.

4. Instruments relating to the profession of the kind of person drawn,
e.g. stethoscopes, dental instruments, chalk, pointers, tongue
depressors, etc., are often included in the drawings. Children seem to
have trouble dissociating a specific kind of person from the "tools of
the trade." They see him or her as someone performing a special function rather than as an ordinary person. Sometimes the *kinds* of tools
drawn (whether their function is associated with pain or not) will give
you a clue about attitude. Sometimes the *size* of the tool relative to the
person will declare its impact on a child. Tools which are particularly
anxiety-provoking may be shaded.

5. Enlarged Drawings
   a) Large dental chairs have been found in the drawings of young
children. These children seem almost overwhelmed by the size of the
chair and perceive themselves as insignificant relative to it.
   b) Large figures have been found in children's drawings of all kinds
of people i.e. doctors, dentists, nurses, teachers. Large figures may indicate that these people are considered significant. Some large figures,
however, are "looming" in quality and suggest aggressivity.
   c) Large hands and fingers are often seen in the drawings of dentists and dental nurses. Since so much of their work involves the hands
used in close proximity to the face of the child, these are emphasized.
   d) Large heads are most frequently seen in the drawings of
teachers. Most likely this reflects the child's attitude to the teacher as a
source of knowledge and a very "smart" person.

6. Needles are found so frequently that they call for a separate listing.
Unlike other instruments which may be associated with either positive
or negative attitudes, they are usually seen as painful and distressing.
In the Klepsch study, they were found most often in the drawings of
nurses. In many cases, size was exaggerated, suggesting that they
loom large in the child's mind.

7. Smiles are generally associated with pleasantness. However,
children have been known to draw smiling, "happy" faces just to
please the examiner. So be alert to the fact that a smile may mask the
real message of the drawing. For instance, a huge, overbearing figure
with needle in hand may be drawn smiling!

8. *Teeth* in drawings are usually associated with aggression. This could apply to drawings of teachers or nurses who may be perceived by the drawer as verbally or generally aggressive. It does not apply, however, in the case of dentists and dental nurses. In these drawings, the teeth are the focus of the professional activities; while they may be a source of concern or anxiety to the child, they do not suggest the kind of aggression associated with drawings of other types of people.

9. *Writing* on drawings gives clues to attitude. Some children include comments in their drawings and draw people "talking." For example, one teacher was drawn with "Johnny, sit down!" coming from her mouth. Objects are often emphasized by labeling, to make sure that the examiner will not mistake them for anything else. Among these are report cards, test schedules, exams, etc. Labeled objects or writing gives clues as to what the child wants to convey and his attitude.

Examples of Drawings

Measuring

Attitudes

DRAWING 1: Drawing of a *teacher* by
third grade girl

The Projection
Overall Impression: Favorable attitude to
school and teacher
Specific Indicators:
- Smile (indicating pleasant personality)
- Pointer (symbol of authority)
- Map, normal classroom accessory (detail shows interest in learning)

DRAWING 2: Drawing of a *teacher* by
third grade girl

The Projection
   Overall Impression: School is restrictive;
   teacher authoritarian
   Specific Indicators:
      • Desk (suggests barrier between teacher
        and students)
      • Written phrase (suggests such com-
        mands may be frequent)

DRAWING 3: Drawing of a *teacher* by
              third grade girl

The Projection
   Overall Impression: Favorable attitude to
   school and learning
   Specific Indicators:
      • Desk (usual classroom accessory)
      • Pencil (usual classroom accessory)
      • Written phrase (speaks for itself)

DRAWING 4: Drawing of a *teacher* by
         third grade boy

The Projection
   Overall Impression: Teacher authoritarian,
   aggressive, punitive
   Specific Indicators:
      • Large ruler or pointer (suggests authori-
        tarian teacher and punishment)
      • Teeth (associated with aggression)
      • Glasses (represent learning and know-
        ledge, or she may wear them)
      • Baselining, i.e., line drawn under feet
        and sole of shoe emphasis (teacher
        makes child feel insecure)

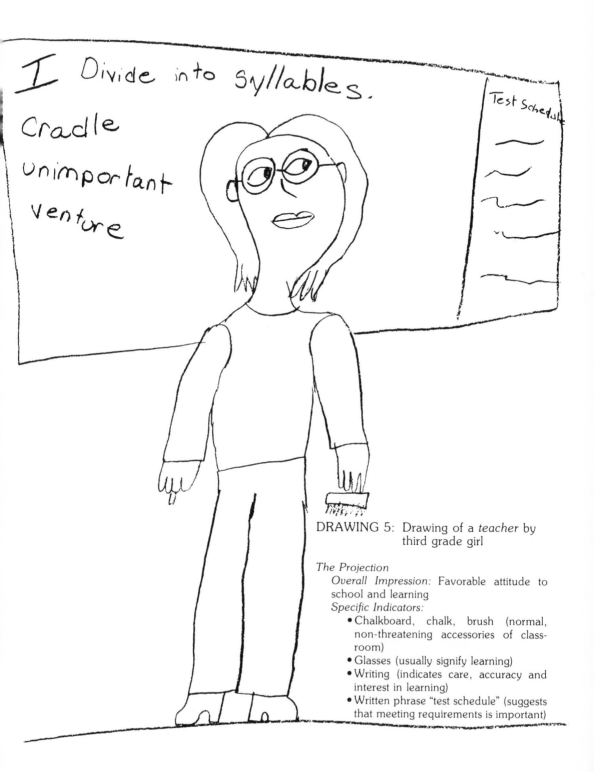

I Divide into syllables.
Cradle
unimportant
venture

Test Schedule

DRAWING 5: Drawing of a *teacher* by third grade girl

The Projection
   Overall Impression: Favorable attitude to school and learning
   Specific Indicators:
      • Chalkboard, chalk, brush (normal, non-threatening accessories of classroom)
      • Glasses (usually signify learning)
      • Writing (indicates care, accuracy and interest in learning)
      • Written phrase "test schedule" (suggests that meeting requirements is important)

DRAWING 6: Drawing of a *teacher* by
third grade boy

The Projection
Overall Impression: Intellectual or cognitive
aspects of learning are important
Specific Indicators:
- Large head (suggests teacher is "smart"
  and knowledge is very important)
- Books on desk (emphasis on learning)
- Smile (nice, friendly teacher)

DRAWING 7: Drawing of a *teacher* by
first grade girl

The Projection
    Overall Impression: Favorable attitude to
    teacher and learning
    Specific Indicators:
        • Very large figure (teacher considered
          extremely significant person)
        • Smile (warm person)
        • Written comments (suggest pleasant,
          respectful relationship, but also suggest
          that compliance is highly valued)

DRAWING 8: Drawing of a *teacher* by
third grade boy

The Projection
   Overall Impression: Cognitive or academic
aspect of learning important; verbal aggression
   Specific Indicators:
      • Teeth (associated with verbal aggres-
        sion)
      • Test schedule (emphasis on learning,
        may be threatening)
      • Glasses (stress intellectual aspect of
        teacher)

DRAWING 9: Drawing of a *doctor* by
eighth grade girl

The Projection
   Overall Impression: Doctor has double stan-
   dard
   Specific Indicators:
      • Clown-like figure (illustrates double
        standard of overweight doctor telling
        someone to lose weight)
      • Written phrase (self-explanatory)
      • Glasses (represent learning and knowl-
        edge)

159

DRAWING 10: Drawing of a *doctor* by
eighth grade boy

The Projection
    Overall Impression: Doctor gives up on
others (and himself?)
    Specific Indicators:
        • Clown-like figure (illustrates double
          standard of doctor failing to take his
          own advice and persuading others to
          take it)
        • Glasses (represent learning and knowl-
          edge)
        • Stethoscope (instrument of the profes-
          sion)

DRAWING 11: Drawing of a *doctor* by
                     eighth grade girl

The Projection
   Overall Impression: Competence and in-
   telligence
   Specific Indicators:
      • Glasses (sign of learning and com-
        petence)
      • Stethoscope (instrument of the profes-
        sion)

DRAWING 12: Drawing of a school *public health nurse* by second grade boy

The Projection
   Overall Impression: Terror of nurse and/or needle
   Specific Indicators:
      • Large needle (instrument of pain which looms large in child's mind)
      • Written phrase and patient's response (these speak for themselves)

Heneedsanedel.

DRAWING 13: Drawing of a school *public health nurse* by fifth
grade boy

The Projection
  Overall Impression: Overbearing, ag-
  gressive, powerful
  Specific Indicators:
    • Large figure (suggests "looming" qual-
      ity)
    • Teeth (indicates aggression)
    • Needle (exaggerated size suggests it
      looms large in child's mind)
    • Stethoscope (tool of the profession,
      represented here almost as a weapon)
    • Cross (worn by some nurses)

DRAWING 14: Drawing of a school *public health nurse* by first
grade boy

The Projection
   Overall Impression: Anxiety over needle
   Specific Indicators:
      • Writing (leaves no doubt about his at-
        titude)

mrs stobbe

DRAWING 15: Drawing of a *dental nurse*
by fifth grade girl

The Projection
   Overall   Impression: Technical   person,
   looms large
   Specific Indicators:
      • Dental instruments (relate to the profes-
        sion)
      • Finger detail, ring
      • Teeth and mouth emphasis (areas of
        concern and professional activities)

DRAWING 16: Drawing of a *dental nurse*
by first grade girl

The Projection
   Overall Impression: Child insignificant and overwhelmed
   Specific Indicators:
      • Large dental chair (some children are overwhelmed by the chair and see themselves as insignificant in comparison)
      • Enlarged teeth on chart (teeth are focus of concern and professional activities)
      • Self drawn tiny

DRAWING 17: Drawing of a *dentist* by
eighth grade boy

The Projection
    Overall Impression: Pain and horror (not
  without humor)
    Specific Indicators:
       • Writing (spells out attitude)
       • Monster-like figure (horror element,
         dentist like Dracula)
       • Teeth (represented as fangs)
       • "Dental" instruments, axe and drill (in-
         struments of torture)

167

DRAWING 18: Drawing of a *dental nurse*
by first grade boy

The Projection
    Overall Impression: Pending doom
    Specific Indicators:
        • Monster-like overhead drill
        • Teeth (area of concern and professional
          activities)
        • Dental instruments (tools of the trade)

DRAWING 19: Drawing of a *dentist* by
first grade boy

The Projection
Overall Impression: Hands and fingers
dominate
Specific Indicators:
- Large hands and fingers (this emphasis
is common in drawings of dentists since
hands are used so close to the child's
face)

DRAWING 20: Drawing of a *dentist* by
first grade boy

The Projection
   Overall Impression: Hand emphasis
   Specific Indicators:
      • Teeth (area of concern and professional
        activity)
      • Large hands (these are emphasized
        since dentist's hands work very close to
        the child's face)

171

DRAWING 21: Drawing of a *dentist* by
fifth grade boy

The Projection
    Overall Impression: Technical person
    Specific Indicators:
        • Teeth (area of concern and professional
          activity)
        • Dental instruments ("tools of the trade")

DRAWING 22: Drawing of a *dentist* by
third grade boy

The Projection
   Overall Impression: Pending doom
   Specific Indicators:
     • Dental instruments ("tools of the trade")
     • Unhappy face of patient
     • Picture of wolf? ready to pounce?

CHAPTER 8

CONCLUSION

In preparing this book, we have reviewed a vast quantity of the existing research relating to the four projective uses of children's HFDs. This literature, coupled with our own clinical experience, has given rise to some very specific ideas which we would like to share with our readers.

The first is in regard to a *multiple measures approach* to assessment in which we firmly believe but which can present some difficulties at times. The research indicates that objective and projective measures often do not correlate well. Sometimes the data we obtain from multiple sources will not add up. For example, the information we gather through observation, from talking to a person, from an objective test and through drawings may be quite contradictory. However, since people are indeed complex beings, this is no cause for dismay. Instead, drawing users should try even harder to pin down what the different sources of information are actually revealing. Verbal methods and objective tests often give us information about *the way a child would like to be* or *the way he would like us to believe he is* – not necessarily about the way he actually is. The information gleaned through observation may be less easy to falsify. It may tell us the way a child really is, but a child may also be trying to impress and behave in ways he thinks people would like him to behave. Observation takes time. Children may not reveal their true identity in a few sessions. By contrast, the information we get from drawings and other projective tests tells us *the way a person really is*. Of all the projective techniques, drawings dig the deepest into the person, even deeper than well-known tests such as the Rorschach and the Thematic Apperception Test (TAT) (Hammer, 1969).

The research makes it quite clear that the *overall impression* gained at first sight of a drawing is more important than any one sign or specific indicator. The warning bears repeating: Never make a judgment about a child on the basis of any one sign. When several signs begin to point in the same direction, we are in a much better position to say something about the child. It is also important to remember that the data derived from a drawing tells us something about the way that person is on a certain day. If we want to check to see if a child is like this all the time, we have to gather drawings over a period of time. By examining several drawings, we can separate enduring characteristics from temporary ones.

While the earlier studies tended to look at the drawings of markedly abnormal groups, the more recent studies, especially those involving children, have been carried out with less atypical groups. We believe that drawings can tell us a great deal about relatively *normal* children who are experiencing the usual kinds of adjustment problems. Group drawings, in particular, can make visible the normal anxieties, jealousies, and frustrations which children experience when relating to others.

We do hope that much more attention will be paid in the future to the studies which view drawings as a measure of *individuality* and *uniqueness*; it is gratifying to note that the humanistic psychologists Combs et al. (1976) and Welch (1979) have also advocated the use of projective tests in this regard. The group of studies dealing with self-esteem and self-concept is particularly interesting, since not much is known about the drawings of those who have high self-esteem or are self-actualized. To date, much of the research effort has been invested in the drawings of the handicapped and those with less than optimal mental health.

The work of Burns and Kaufman, originators of the Kinetic Family Drawing technique, has sparked renewed interest in research relating to both family and school group drawings. Kinetic instructions can produce drawings rich in projective content. In group drawings, which focus on relationships, this is especially valuable, since difficulty with relationships is often the reason children are referred. In these times of marital discord, single-parent families, high mobility, second marriages, etc., it is extremely important to have an insight into children's perceptions of themselves relative to others. We were impressed with studies in which both parents and children were required to draw their families in an effort to obtain the perceptions of all family members.

Most of the research so far has zeroed in on the use of HFDs to measure personality. Very little has been done in regard to drawings to assess *attitudes*. We strongly believe this is a field for future study. We ourselves have done some preliminary work in examining children's attitudes toward doctors, dentists, nurses, dental nurses and teachers. Could this work not be extended to attitudes toward policemen, firemen, politicians, postmen, presidents, or prime ministers? The possibilities seem endless. The use of kinetic drawings could add another dimension. We feel a great deal could be learned about the types of activities children perceive significant others carrying out by asking them to draw, say, a policeman *doing something.*

Drawings are particularly useful for children with *verbal expressive problems.* They could serve as a vehicle of expression for *deaf* children. Those with language or articulation disorders and those who stutter may find verbal situations anxiety-provoking and might be more apt to express themselves graphically. We think it is important, therefore, for those who work with these children to have some training in drawing interpretation so they can understand what the children are saying in their drawings.

Some drawings, particularly the *family* drawings, may speed up progress in family therapy or assist with parent counseling if they are shown to the parents. A picture is worth a thousand words, according to an old adage. Burns (1980) reports that a father joined AA after examining his child's kinetic family drawing which showed the destructive effect his drinking had on family functioning. Klepsch has found that parents can quickly change their attitudes toward a particular child when they understand how he sees himself in the family. For example, one child drew his younger sister much larger and with considerably more detail than any other person in his family. When the parents saw the drawing, they were quite taken aback, but it served as a stimulus for discussion about why this child viewed his sister as being more significant than others. Again, parents on seeing their child's drawing of the family may say that the way the child sees himself in the family is not the way things really are. However, what is important is the child's perception; while he may not see the family as the parents do, or see it as it actually is, the way he sees himself in the family must be acknowledged. We must look at his perceptions as seen in the drawing and try to find why he views the situation as he does. The drawing has provided us with a valuable clue to his perceptions.

We have a word of caution for potential users of drawings about giving drawing instructions. The instructor's attitude can affect the kind of drawings obtained! Although the instructions are simple and straightforward, they can convey a disinterested or cynical attitude, which is

176

quickly picked by the children. The result will be drawings which are poorly done and lacking in projective content.

Finally, we deplore recent trends which have deemphasized training in projective assessment techniques. In the past, psychologists were trained in projective methods. Unfortunately, the current preoccupation with behaviorism and behavior modification has led many training institutions to drop courses in this area. It can no longer be assumed that all psychologists have either the interest or skills to use drawings. We therefore feel that people other than psychologists, professionals who work with children, should be prepared to acquaint themselves with what drawings have to say.

REFERENCES

Adler, P. T. Evaluation of the figure drawing technique: Reliability factorial structure, and diagnostic usefulness. *Journal of Consulting and Clinical Psychology*, 1970, *35*, 52-57.

Anastasi, A. & Foley, J. P. An analysis of spontaneous drawings by children in different cultures. *Journal of Applied Psychology*, 1936, *20*, 680-726.

Apfeldorf, M., Walter, C. L., Kaimen, B. D., Smith, W. J. & Arnett, W. A method for the evaluation of affective association to figure drawings. *Journal of Personality Assessment*, 1974, *38*, 441-449.

Arkell, R. Naive prediction of pathology from human figure drawings. *Journal of School Psychology*, 1976, *14*, 114-117(a).

Arkell, R. Adults' representations of children's human figure drawings. *Perceptual and Motor Skills*, 1976, *43*, 958(b).

Arlin, M. & Hills, J. *Arlin-Hills Attitude Survey*. Jacksonville, Ill.: Psychologists and Educators Inc., 1976.

Bachara, G. H. & Zaba, J. N. Psychological effects of visual training. *Academic Therapy*, 1976, *12*, 99-104.

Bachara, G., Zaba, J. & Raskin, L. Human figures drawings and L. D. children. *Academic Therapy*, 1975, *11*, 217-222.

Ball, S. *Assessing the attitudes of young children toward school*. Head Start Collection Report. Office of Child Development, Department of Health, Education and Welfare. Washington, D.C.: U.S. Government Printing Office, 1971.

Bellamy, E. & Daly, W. C. The height of figure drawings related to IQ, sex and CA in mental retardates. *Journal of Clinical Psychology*, 1969, *25*, 206-207.

Bender, L. The Goodenough test (drawing a man) in chronic encephalitis in children. *Journal of Nervous and Mental Disease*, 1940, *91*, 277-286.

Berryman, E. The self portrait: A suggested extension of the HTP. *Perceptual and Motor Skills*, 1959, *9*, 411-414.

Bieliauskas, V. J. Sexual identification in children's drawings of human figure. *Journal of Clinical Psychology*, 1960, *16*, 42-44.

Bieliauskas, V. J. & Bristow, R. B. The effect of formal art training upon the quantitative scores of the H-T-P. *Journal of Clinical Psychology*, 1959, *15*, 57-59.

Black, F. W. Factors related to human figure drawing size in children. *Perceptual and Motor Skills*, 1972, *35*, 902.

Blum, L. H. Darkness in an enlightened era: Women's drawings of their sexual organs. *Psychological Reports*, 1978, *42*, 867-873.

Blum, R. H. The validity of the Machover DAP technique. *Journal of Clinical Psychology*, 1954, *10*, 120-125.

Brannigan, G., Margolis, H. & Moran, P. Cognitive tempo and children's human figure drawings. *Perceptual and Motor Skills*, 1979, *49*, 414.

Britain, S. D. Effect of manipulation of children's affect on their family drawings. *Journal of Projective Techniques and Personality Assessment*, 1970, *34*, 234-237.

Bromberg, W. & Hutchinson, S. H. Self image of the American Indian. *International Journal of Social Psychiatry*, 1974, *20*, 39-44.

Brown, E. V. Sexual self-identification as reflected in children's drawings when asked to "Draw-A-Person". *Perceptual and Motor Skills*, 1979, *49*, 35-38.

Brumback, R. A. Characteristics of the Inside-Of-The-Body test drawings performed by normal school children. *Perceptual and Motor Skills*, 1977, *44*, 703-708.

Brumback, R. A., Bertorini, T. & Liberman, J. Inside-Of-The-Body test drawings performed by patients with neuromuscular diseases: A preliminary report. *Perceptual and Motor Skills*, 1978, *47*, 155-160.

Buck, J. N. The H-T-P technique: A qualitative and quantitative scoring manual. *Journal of Clinical Psychology*, 1948, *4*, 317-396.

Buck, J. N. *The House-Tree-Person (H-T-P Manual Supplement)*. Beverly Hills, Ca.: Western Psychological Services, 1964.

Buck, J. N. & Hammer, E. F. (Eds.). *Advances in House-Tree-Person Techniques: Variations and Applications*. Los Angeles, Ca.: Western Psychological Services, 1969.

Burns, C. J. & Velicer, W. F. Art instruction and the Goodenough-Harris drawing test in fifth graders. *Psychology in the Schools*, 1977, *14*, 109-112.

Burns, R. C. What children are telling us in their human figure drawings. *Venture Forth*, 1980, *11*, 6-11.

Burns, R. C. *Self-growth in families: Kinetic Family Drawings (K-F-D) research and application*. New York: Brunner/Mazel, 1982.

Burns, R. C. & Kaufman, S. H. *Kinetic Family Drawings (K-F-D)*. New York: Brunner/Mazel, 1970.

Burns, R. C. & Kaufman, S. H. *Action, styles and symbols in Kinetic Family Drawings (K-F-D): An interpretive manual*. New York: Brunner/Mazel, 1972.

Burton, R. V. Cross-sex identity in Barbados. *Developmental Psychology*, 1972, *6*, 365-374.

Centers, L. & Centers, R. A comparison of the body images of amputee and non-amputee children as revealed in figure drawings. *Journal of Projective Techniques*, 1963, *27*, 158-165.

Cohen, S. M., Money, J. & Uhlenhuth, E. H. A computer study of selected features of self-and-other drawings by 385 children. *Journal of Learning Disabilities*, 1972, *5*, 145-155.

Combs, A. W. Personal communication, April 10, 1979.

Combs, A. W., Richards, A. C. & Richards, F. *Perceptual Psychology*, New York: Harper & Row, 1976.

Cook, S. W. & Selltiz, C. A multiple-indicator approach to attitude measurement. *Psychological Bulletin*, 1964, *62*, 36-55.

Coopersmith, S., Sakai, D., Beardslee, B. & Coopersmith, A. Figure drawings as an expression of self esteem. *Journal of Personality Assessment*, 1976, *40*, 370-375.

Coyle, F. A. & Eisenman, R. Santa Claus drawings by Negro and White children. *Journal of Social Psychology*, 1970, *80*, 201-205.

Coyle, R. T., Clance, P. R. & Joesting, J. Kinesthetic enrichment and Goodenough-Harris Draw-a-Man scores of black children from lower socioeconomic background. *Perceptual and Motor Skills*, 1977, *45*, 201-202.

Cressen, R. Artistic quality of drawings and judge's evaluations of the DAP. *Journal of Personality Assessment,* 1975, *39,* 132-137.

Dalby, J. T. & Vale, H. L. Self esteem and children's human figure drawings. *Perceptual and Motor Skills,* 1977, *44,* 1279-1282.

Daoud, F. S. First drawn pictures: A cross cultural investigation. *Journal of Personality Assessment,* 1976, *40,* 376-377.

Davis, C. J. & Hoopes, J. L. Comparison of House-Tree-Person drawings of young deaf and hearing children. *Journal of Personality Assessment,* 1975, *39,* 28-33.

De Martino, M. F. Human figure drawings by mentally retarded males. *Journal of Clinical Psychology,* 1954, *10,* 241-244.

Dennis, W. Handwriting conventions as determinants of human figure drawings. *Journal of Consulting Psychology,* 1958, *22,* 293-295.

Dennis, W. *Group values through children's drawings.* New York: John Wiley & Sons, 1966.

Dennis, W. Racial changes in Negro drawings. *Journal of Psychology,* 1968, *69,* 129-130.

Dennis, W. & Raskin, E. Further evidence concerning the effect of handwriting habits upon the location of drawings. *Journal of Consulting Psychology,* 1960, *24,* 548-549.

Dennis, W. & Uras, A. The religious content of human figure drawings made by nuns. *Journal of Psychology,* 1965, *61,* 263-266.

Deren, S. An empirical evaluation of the validity of the Draw-a-Family test. *Journal of Clinical Psychology,* 1975, *31,* 47-52.

Di Leo, J. H. *Children's drawings as diagnostic aids.* New York: Brunner/Mazel, 1973.

Dillard, H. K. & Landsman, M. The Evanston Early Identification Scale: Prediction of school problems from the human figure drawings of kindergarten children. *Journal of Clinical Psychology,* 1968, *24,* 227-228.

Dunleavy, R. A., Hanson, J. L. & Szasz, C. W. Early kindergarten identification of academically not-ready children by use of human figure drawing developmental score. *Psychology in the Schools,* 1981, *18,* 35-38.

Ekman, P. & Friesen, W. V. The repertoire of nonverbal behavior: Categories, origins, usage, and coding. *Semiotica,* 1969, *1,* 49-98.

Engle, P. L. & Suppes, J. S. The relation between human figure drawings and test anxiety in children. *Journal of Projective Techniques and Personality Assessment,* 1970, *34,* 223-231.

Faterson, H. F. & Witkin, H. A. Longitudinal study of development of the body concept. *Developmental Psychology,* 1970, *2,* 429-438.

Fisher, G. M. Nudity in human figure drawings. *Journal of Clinical Psychology,* 1961, *17,* 307-308.

Fox, C., Davidson, K., Lighthall, F., Waite, R. & Sarason, S. B. Human figure drawings of high and low anxious children. *Child Development,* 1958, *29,* 297-301.

Frankenburg, W. K. & Dodds, J. B. *The Denver Developmental Screening Test-Revised.* Denver, LADOCA, 1975.

Fuller, G. R., Preuss, M. & Hawkins, W. F. The validity of the human figure drawings with disturbed and normal children. *Journal of School Psychology,* 1970, *8,* 54-56.

Gardiner, H. W. A cross cultural comparison of hostility in children's drawings. *Journal of Social Psychology,* 1969, *79,* 261-263.

Gardiner, H. W. Human figure drawings as indicators of value development among Thai children. *Journal of Cross-Cultural Psychology,* 1974, *5,* 124-130.

Gardner, H. *Artful Scribbles.* New York: Basic Books, 1980.

Goodenough, F. L. *Measurement of intelligence by drawings.* New York: Harcourt, Brace & World, 1926.

181

Green, M. & Levitt, E. E. Constriction of body image in children with congenital heart disease. *Pediatrics*, 1962, *29*, 438-441.

Griffith, A. V. & Peyman, D. A. R. Eye-ear emphasis on the DAP as indicating ideas of reference. *Journal of Consulting Psychology*, 1959, *23*, 560.

Hall, L. P. & Ladriere, M. L. A comparative study of diagnostic potential and efficency of six scoring systems applied to children's figure drawings. *Psychology in the Schools*, 1970, *7*, 244-247.

Hammer, E. Personal Contact, 1980.

Hammer, E. F. Negro and white children's personality adjustment as revealed by comparison of their drawings (HTP). *Journal of Clinical Psychology*, 1953, *9*, 7-10.

Hammer, E. F. The role of the H-T-P in the prognostic battery. *Journal of Clinical Psychology*, 1953, *9*, 371-374.

Hammer, E. F. Critique of Swensen's "Empirical evaluations of human figure drawings." *Journal of Projective Techniques*, 1959, *23*, 30-32.

Hammer, E. F. DAP: Back against the wall? *Journal of Consulting and Clinical Psychology*, 1969, *33*, 151-156. (a)

Hammer, E. F. Hierarchical organization of personality and the H-T-P, achromatic and chromatic. In Buck, J. N. & Hammer, E. F. (Eds.) *Advances in House-Tree-Person Techniques: Variations and Applications*. Los Angeles, Cal.: Western Psychological Services, 1969, 1-35. (b)

Hammer, M. & Kaplan, A. M. The reliability of sex of first figure drawn by children. *Journal of Clinical Psychology*, 1964, *20*, 251-252. (a)

Hammer, M. & Kaplan, A. M. Reliability of profile and front-facing directions in children's drawings. *Child Development*, 1964, *35*, 973-977. (b)

Hammer, M. & Kaplan, A. M. The reliability of children's human figure drawings. *Journal of Clinical Psychology*, 1966, *22*, 316-319.

Handler, L. & Reyher, J. The effects of stress on the Draw-a-Person test. *Journal of Consulting Psychology*. 1964, *28*, 259-264.

Handler, L. & Reyher, J. Figure drawing anxiety indexes: A review of the literature. *Journal of Projective Techniques and Personality Assessment*, 1965, *29*, 305-313.

Hare, A. P. & Hare, R. T. The Draw-a-Group test. *The Journal of Genetic Psychology*, 1956, *89*, 51-59.

Harris, D. B. *Children's drawings as measures of intellectual maturity*. New York: Harcourt, Brace & World, 1963.

Harris, D. B. & Roberts, J. *Intellectual maturity of children: Demographic and sociometric factors* (DHEW, Vital and Health Statistics Series 11, No. 116). Washington, D.C.: U.S. Government Printing Office, 1972.

Heinrich, P. & Triebe, J. K. Sex preferences in children's human figure drawings. *Journal of Personality Assessment*, 1972, *36*, 263-267.

Henderson, N. B., Butler, B. V., Goffeney, B., Saito, C. H. & Clarkson, Q. D. Sex of person drawn by Japanese, Navajo, American white and negro seven-year-olds. *Journal of Personality Assessment*, 1971, *35*, 261-264.

Hiler, E. W. & Nesvig, D. An evaluation of criteria used by clinicians to infer pathology from figure drawings. *Journal of Consulting Psychology*, 1965, *29*, 520-529.

Hulse, W. C. Childhood conflict expressed through family drawings. *Journal of Projective Techniques*, 1952, *16*, 66-79.

Hulse, W. C. The emotionally disturbed child draws his family. *Quarterly Journal of Child Behavior*, 1951, *3*, 152-174.

Ilg, F. L. & Ames, L. B. *School readiness: Behavior tests used at the Gesell Institute*. New York: Harper & Row, 1978.

Jacobson, D. A. *A study of Kinetic Family Drawings of public school children ages six through nine*. Unpublished doctoral dissertation, University of Cincinnati, 1973.

Johnson, F. A. & Greenberg, R. P. Quality of drawings as a factor in the interpretation of figure drawings. *Journal of Personality Assessment*, 1978, *42*, 489-495.

Johnson, J. H. Note on the validity of Machover's indicators of anxiety. *Perceptual and Motor Skills*, 1971, *33*, 126.(a)

Johnson, J. H. Upper left hand placement of human figure drawings as an indicator of anxiety. *Journal of Personality Assessment*, 1971, *35*, 336-337.(b)

Johnson, O. G. & Wawrzaszek, F. Psychologists' judgments of physical handicap from H-T-P drawings. *Journal of Consulting Psychology*, 1961, *25*, 284-287.

Jolles, I. Some advances in interpretation of the chromatic phase of the H-T-P. *Journal of Clinical Psychology*, 1957, *13*, 81-83.

Jolles, I. *A catalog for the qualitative interpretation of the House-Tree-Person (H-T-P)*. Los Angeles: Western Psychological Services, 1971.

Kahn, S. B. A comparative study of assessing children's school-related attitudes. *Journal of Educational Measurement*, 1978, *15*, 59-66.

Klepsch, M. E. *A comparison of children's drawings of dentists and dental nurses*. Unpublished study, North Battleford, Saskatchewan, 1975.

Klepsch, M. E. *A Validation Study of the Draw-a-Teacher Technique on Third Grade Children*. Unpublished doctoral dissertation, University of Northern Colorado, 1979.

Klepsch, M. E. *Drawings as a measure of children's attitudes to doctors, dentists and nurses*. Unpublished study, North Battleford, Saskatchewan, 1980.

Klepsch, M. E. *A Study to Assess the Cultural Values of Canadian Cree Children Kindergarten through Grade Nine*. Unpublished study, North Battleford, Saskatchewan, 1981.

Klopfer, W. G. & Taulbee, E. S. Projective tests. In M. R. Rosenzweig and L. M. Porter (Eds.), *Annual Review of Psychology* (Vol 27). Palo Alto: Annual Reviews Inc., 1976.

Koppitz, E. M. Teacher's attitude and children's performance on the Bender Gestalt Test and human figure drawings. *Journal of Clinical Psychology*, 1960, *16*, 204-208.

Koppitz, E. M. Emotional indicators on human figure drawings of children: A validation study. *Journal of Clinical Psychology*, 1966, *22*, 313-315.(a)

Koppitz, E. M. Emotional indicators on human figure drawings of shy and aggressive children. *Journal of Clinical Psychology*, 1966, *22*, 466-469.(b)

Koppitz, E. M. *Psychological evaluation of children's human figure drawings*. New York: Grune & Stratton, 1968.

Koppitz, E. M. Emotional indicators on human figure drawings of boys and girls from lower and middle-class backgrounds. *Journal of Clinical Psychology*, 1969, *25*, 432-434.

Kuhlman, T. L. A validation study of the Draw-A-Person as a measure of racial identity acceptance. *Journal of Personality Assessment*, 1979, *43*, 5.

Kuhlman, T. L. & Bieliauskas, V. J. A comparison of Black and White Adolescents on the H-T-P. *Journal of Clinical Psychology*, 1976, *32*, 728-731.

Kutnick, P. Children's drawings of their classrooms: Development and social maturity. *Child Study Journal*, 1978, *8*, 175-185.

Laosa, L. M., Swartz, J. D. & Diaz-Guerrero, R. Perceptual-cognitive and personality development of Mexican and Anglo-American children as measured by human figure drawings. *Developmental Psychology*, 1974, *10*, 131-139.

Lawton, M. J. & Sechrest, L. Figure drawings by young boys from father-present and father-absent homes. *Journal of Clinical Psychology*, 1962, *18*, 304-305.

Leichtman, S. Artists' simulation of preschoolers' human figure drawings. *Perceptual and Motor Skills*, 1979, *49*, 18.

Levenberg, S. B. Professional training, psychodiagnostic skill, and kinetic family drawings. *Journal of Personality Assessment*, 1975, *39*, 389-393.

Lingren, R. H. An attempted replication of emotional indicators in human drawings by shy and aggressive children. *Psychological Reports*, 1971, *29*, 35-38.

Litt, S. & Margoshes, A. Sex-change in successive Draw-a-Person Tests. *Journal of Clinical Psychology*, 1966, *22*, 470.

183

Loney, J. Clinical aspects of the Loney Draw-a-Car test: Enuresis and encopresis. *Journal of Personality Assessment,* 1971, *35,* 265-274.

Loney, J. The sun as a measure of dependency in children's drawings. *Journal of Clinical Psychology,* 1971, *27,* 513-514.

Lourenso, S. V., Greenberg, J. W. & Davidson, H. H. Personality characteristics revealed in drawings of deprived children who differ in school achievement. *Journal of Educational Research,* 1965, *59,* 63-67.

Machover, K. *Personality Projection in the drawings of a human figure.* Springfield: Charles C. Thomas, 1949.

Machover, K. Human figure drawings of children. *Journal of Projective Techniques,* 1953, *17,* 85-91.

Mangum, M. E. *Familial identification in Black, Anglo and Chicano mentally retarded children using Kinetic Family Drawing.* Unpublished doctoral dissertation, University of Northern Colorado, 1975.

Marzolf, S. S. & Kirchner, J. H. Personality traits and color choices for house-tree-person drawings. *Journal of Clinical Psychology,* 1973, *29,* 240-245.

McHugh, A. F. H-T-P proportion and perspective in Negro, Puerto Rican and White children. *Journal of Clinical Psychology,* 1963, *19,* 312-313.

McHugh, A. F. Age associations in children's figure drawings. *Journal of Clinical Psychology,* 1965, *21,* 429-431.

McHugh, A. F. Children's figure drawings in neurotic and conduct disturbances. *Journal of Clinical Psychology,* 1966, *22,* 219-221.

McMeniman, J. H. The use of graphic art expression in the measurement of attitudes. In *Attitudes Handbook,* American Council on Education, 1951.

McPhee, J. P. & Wenger, K. W. Kinetic-Family-Drawing styles and emotionally disturbed childhood behavior. *Journal of Personality Assessment,* 1976, *40,* 487-491.

Miller, S. R., Sabatino, D. A. & Miller, T. L. Influence of training in visual perceptual discrimination on drawings by children. *Perceptual and Motor Skills,* 1977, *44,* 479-487.

Morris, W. W. Ontogenetic changes in adolescence reflected by the drawing-human-figures technique. *American Journal of Orthopsychiatry,* 1955, *25,* 720-728.

Mott, S. M. Concept of mother: A study of four- and five-year-old children. *Child Development,* 1954, *25,* 99-106.

Myers, D. V. Toward an objective evaluation procedure of the Kinetic Family Drawings (KFD). *Journal of Personality Assessment,* 1978, *42,* 358-365.

Nathan, S. Body image in chronically obese children as reflected in figure drawings. *Journal of Personality Assessment,* 1974, *37,* 456-463.

O'Brien, R. P. & Patton, W. F. Development of an objective scoring method for the Kinetic Family Drawing. *Journal of Personality Assessment,* 1974, *38,* 156-164.

Offord, D. R. & Aponte, J. F. A comparison of drawings and sentence completion responses of congenital heart children with normal children. *Journal of Projective Techniques and Personality Assessment,* 1970, *34,* 57-62.

Ogden, D. P. *Psychodiagnostics and personality assessment: A handbook* (2nd ed.). Los Angeles: Western Psychological Services, 1975.

Ottenbacher, K. An investigation of self-concept and body image in the mentally retarded. *Journal of Clinical Psychology,* 1981, *37,* 415-418.

Patalano, F. Height on the Draw-a-Person: Comparison of figure drawings of black and white male drug abusers. *Perceptual and Motor Skills,* 1977, *44,* 1187-1190.

Pate, R. H. & Nichols, W. R. A scoring guide for the Koppitz system of evaluating children's human figure drawings. *Psychology in the Schools,* 1971, *8,* 55-56.

Phelan, H. M. The incidence and possible significance of the drawing of female figures by sixth-grade boys in response to the Draw-a-Person test. *Psychiatric Quarterly,* 1964, *38,* 488-503.

Phillips, S. Children's perceptions of health and disease. *Canadian Family Physician,* 1980, *26,* 1171-1174.

Pihl, R. O. & Nimrod, G. The reliability and validity of the Draw-a-Peson test in I.Q. and personality assessment. *Journal of Clinical Psychology,* 1976, *32,* 470-472.

Porter, R. B. & Cattell, R. B. *Children's Personality Questionnaire.* Champaign, Ill.: Institute for Personality and Ability Testing, 1963.

Precker, J. A. Painting and drawing in personality assessment. *Journal of Projective Techniques,* 1950, *14,* 262-286.

Prout, H. T. & Phillips, P. D. A clinical note: The Kinetic School Drawing. *Psychology in the Schools,* 1974, *11,* 303-306.

Prytula, R. & Leigh, G. Absolute and relative drawing size in institutionalized orphans. *Journal of Clinical Psychology,* 1972, *28,* 377-379.

Prytula, R. E. & Hiland, D. N. Analysis of General Anxiety Scale for Children and Draw-a-Person measures of general anxiety level of elementary school children. *Perceptual and Motor Skills,* 1975, *41,* 995-1007.

Prytula, R. E., Phelps, M. R., Morrissey, E. F. & Davis, S. F. Figure drawing size as a reflection of self-concept or self-esteem. *Journal of Clinical Psychology,* 1978, *34,* 207-214.

Prytula, R. E. & Thompson, N. D. Analysis of emotional indicators in human figure drawings as related to self esteem. *Perceptual and Motor Skills,* 1973, *37,* 795-802.

Pustel, G., Sternlicht, M. & De Respinis, M. Institutionalized retardates' animal drawings: Their meaning and significance. *Journal of Genetic Psychology,* 1972, *120,* 103-109.

Rabin, A. I. & Limuaco, J. A. Sexual differentiation of American and Filipino children as reflected in the Draw-a-Person test. *Journal of Social Psychology,* 1959, *50,* 207-211.

Raskin, L. M. & Pitcher-Baker, G. Kinetic Family Drawings by children with perceptual-motor delays. *Journal of Learning Disabilities,* 1977, *10,* 370-374.

Reynolds, C. R. A quick-scoring guide to the interpretation of children's Kinetic Family Drawings (KFD). *Psychology in the Schools,* 1978, *15,* 489-492.

Reznikoff, M. & Reznikoff H. R. The family drawing test: A comparative study of children's drawings. *Journal of Clinical Psychology,* 1956, *12,* 167-169.

Reznikoff, M. & Tomblen, D. The use of human figure drawings in the diagnosis of organic pathology. *Journal of Consulting Psychology,* 1956, *20,* 467-470.

Ribler, R. I. Diagnostic prediction from emphasis on the eye and the ear in human figure drawings. *Journal of Consulting Psychology,* 1957, *21,* 223-225.

Rierdan, J. & Koff, E. Sexual ambiguity in children's human figure drawings. *Journal of Personality Assessment,* 1981, *45,* 256-257.

Rimoldi, H. J., Insua, A. M. & Erdmann, J. B. Personality dimensions as assessed by projective and verbal instruments. *Journal of Clinical Psychology,* 1975, *31,* 529-539.

Roback, H. B. Human figure drawings: Their utility in the clinical psychologist's armamentarium for personality assessment. *Psychological Bulletin,* 1968, *70,* 1-19.

Saarni, C. & Azara, A. Developmental analysis of human figure drawings in adolescence, young adulthood and middle age. *Journal of Personality Assessment,* 1977, *41,* 31-38.

Sarason, S., Davidson, K., Lighthall, F., Write, R. & Ruebush, B. *Anxiety in elementary school children.* New York: Wiley, 1960.

Schildkrout, M. S., Shenker, I. R. & Sonnenblick, M. *Human figure drawings in adolescence.* New York: Brunner/Mazel, 1972.

Schneider, G. B. *A preliminary validation study of the Kinetic School Drawing.* Unpublished doctoral dissertation, University of Northern Colorado, 1977.

Schofield, J. W. An exploratory study of the Draw-a-Person as a measure of racial identity. *Perceptual and Motor Skills,* 1978, *46,* 311-321.

Schornstein, H. M. & Derr, J. The many applications of Kinetic Family Drawings in child abuse. *The British Journal of Projective Psychology and Personality Study*, 1978, *23*, 33-35.

Shanan, J. Intraindividual response variability in figure drawing tasks. *Journal of Projective Techniques*, 1962, *26*, 105-111.

Shearn, C. R. & Russell, K. R. Use of the family drawing technique for studying parent-child interaction. *Journal of Projective Techniques and Personality Assessment*, 1970, *34*, 35-44.

Sherman, L. J. The influence of artistic quality on judgments of patient and non-patient status from human figure drawings. *Journal of Projective Techniques*, 1958, *22*, 338-340.

Silverstein, A. B. & Robinson, H. A. The representation of orthopedic disability in children's figure drawings. *Journal of Consulting Psychology*, 1956, *20*, 333-341.

Sims, C. A. Kinetic Family Drawings and the Family Relations Indicator. *Journal of Clinical Psychology*, 1974, *30*, 87-88.

Smart, R. C. & Smart, M. S. Group values shown in pre-adolescents' drawings in five English-speaking countries. *Journal of Social Psychology*, 1975, *97*, 23-27.

Snyder, R. T. & Gaston, D. E. The figure drawing of the first grade child – Item analysis and comparison with Koppitz norms. *Journal of Clinical Psychology*, 1970, *26*, 377-383.

Solar, D., Bruehl, D. & Kovacs, A. The Draw-a-Person test: Social conformity or artistic ability? *Journal of Clinical Psychology*, 1970, *26*, 524-525.

Sonnenberg, E. & Venham, L. Human figure drawings as a measure of the child's response to dental visits. *Journal of Dentistry for Children*, 1977, *44*, 438-442.

Sopchak, A. L. Anxiety indicators on the Draw-a-Person test for clinic and non-clinic boys and their parents. *Journal of Psychology*, 1970, *76*, 251-260.

Springer, N. N. A study of the drawings of maladjusted and adjusted children. *The Journal of Genetic Psychology*, 1941, *58*, 131-138.

Stavrianos, B. K. Emotional and organic characteristics in drawings of deficient readers. *Journal of Learning Disabilities*, 1970, *10*, 488-501.

Striker, G. Actuarial, naive clinical, and sophisticated clinical prediction of pathology from figure drawings. *Journal of Consulting Psychology*, 1967, *31*, 492-494.

Sturner, R. A. & Rothbaum, F. The effect of stress on children's human figure drawings. *Journal of Clinical Psychology*, 1980, *36*, 324-331.

Swartz, J. D., Laosa, L. M. & McGavern, M. L. Spatial placement of human figure drawings as an indicator of cognitive and personality characteristics among normal young adolescents. *Journal of Consulting and Clinical Psychology*, 1976, *44*, 307-308.

Swenson, C. H. Empirical evaluations of human figure drawings. *Psychological Bulletin*, 1957, *54*, 431-466.

Swenson, C. H. Empirical evaluations of human figure drawings. *Psychological Bulletin*, 1968, *70*, 20-44.

Szasz, C. W., Baade, L. E. & Paskewicz, C. W. Emotional and developmental aspects of human figure drawings in predicting school readiness. *Journal of School Psychology*, 1980, *18*, 67-73.

Tait, C. D. & Ascher, R. C. Inside-of-the-Body test. A preliminary report. *Psychosomatic Medicine*, 1955, *17*, 139-148.

Thomson, D. S. and the Editors of Time-Life Books. *Language.* New York: Time-Life, 1975, p. 95.

Thurber, S. Changes in Navajo responses to the Draw-a-Man test. *The Journal of Social Psychology*, 1976, *99*, 139-140.

Tolor, A. Teachers' judgments of the popularity of children from their human figure drawings. *Journal of Clinical Psychology*, 1955, *11*, 158-162.

Tolor, A. & Tolor B. Children's figure drawings and changing attitudes toward sex roles. *Psychological Reports*, 1974, *34*, 343-349.

Torrance, P. Projective and other non-structured techniques. In *Attitudes Handbook*. American Council on Education, 1951.

Uhlin, D. M. & Dickson, J. D. The effect of figure-ground reversal in H-T-D drawings by spastic cerebral palsied children. *Journal of Clinical Psychology*, 1970, *26*, 87-88.

Urban, W. H. *The Draw-a-Person catalogue for interpretative analysis*. Los Angeles: Western Psychological Services, 1963.

Verinis, J. S., Lichtenberg, E. F. & Henrich, L. The Draw-a-Person in the rain technique: Its relationship to diagnostic category and other personality indicators. *Journal of Clinical Psychology*, 1974, *30*, 407-414.

Wagner, R. F. Human figure drawings of LD children. *Academic Therapy*, 1980, *16*, 37-41.

Wanderer, Z. W. Validity of clinical judgments based on human figure drawings. *Journal of Consulting and Clinical Psychology*, 1969, *33*, 143-150.

Wawrzaszek, F., Johnson, O. G. & Sciera, J. L. A comparison of H-T-P responses of handicapped and non-handicapped children. *Journal of Clinical Psychology*, 1958, *14*, 160-162.

Webb, E. J., Campbell, D. T., Schwartz, R. D. & Sechrest, L. *Unobstrusive measures: Nonreactive research in the social sciences*. Chicago: Rand McNally, 1966.

Weider, A. & Nolles, P. A. Objective studies of children's drawings of human figures: Sex, age, intelligence. *Journal of Clinical Psychology*, 1953, *9*, 20-23.

Welch, I. D. Personal communication, May, 1979.

Welch, I. D., Flannigan, M. W. & Rave, E. J. Children's drawings: What they tell us about the way kids see schools. *The Innovator*, 1971, *2*, 28-29.

Whitmyre, J. W. The significance of artistic excellence in the judgment of adjustment inferred from human figure drawings. *Journal of Consulting Psychology*, 1953, *17*, 421-424.

Wilee, C. T. & Davis, S. F. Level of self esteem and size of human figure drawing as a function of group vs. individual administration. *Psychological Reports*, 1976, *39*, 130.

Wysocki, B. A. & Whitney, E. Body image of crippled children as seen in Draw-a-Person test behavior. *Perceptual and Motor Skills*, 1965, *21*, 499-504.

Wysocki, B. A. & Wysocki, A. C. The body image of normal and retarded children. *Journal of Clinical Psychology*, 1973, *29*, 7-10.

Ziv, A. & Shechori, H. Human figure drawing as a measure of social adjustment in school. *Journal of School Psychology*, 1970, *8*, 152-153.

Zuk, G. H. Relation of mental age to size of figure on the Draw-a-Person test. *Perceptual and Motor Skills*, 1962, *14*, 410.

INDEX

Burns, C.J., 31, 180n.
Burns, R.C., vi, viin., 79-81, 85, 88, 175, 176, 180n.
Burton, R.V., 117, 180n.
Butler, B.V., 117, 182n.
Buttons in drawings, 45, 53, 56, 63, 66, 67, 70, 105

Campbell, D.T., 11, 187n.
Canadian Broadcasting Company, 6
Cattell, R.B., 22, 185n.
Centers, L., 28, 180n.
Centers, R., 28, 180n.
Cerebral palsy, 55
Children's Manifest Anxiety Scale (CMAS), 81
Children's Personality Questionnaire, 22
Clance, P.R., 30, 180n.
Clarkson, Q.D., 117, 182n.
Clothing in drawings, 113, 118-19, 122, 128, 132, 134, 141
Clown drawings, 45, 63, 146, 159, 160
Cohen, S.M., 82, 180n.
Color in drawings, 35, 77, 116, 120
Combs, A.W., 175, 180n.
Congenital heart disease and drawings, 29, 40
Cook, S.W., 11, 180n.
Cooperation in drawings, 113, 115, 119, 122, 124, 126, 132, 133, 141
Coopersmith, A., 26, 180n.
Coopersmith, S., 26, 180n.
Coopersmith Self-Esteem Inventory, 26, 81
Cowboy drawings, 45
Coyle, F.A., 116, 180n.
Coyle, R.T., 30, 180n.
Cressen, R., 32, 181n.
Culture and drawings, 112-14

Dalby, J.T., 26, 38, 181n.
Daly, W.C., 29, 179n.
Daoud, F.S., 117, 181n.
Davidson, H.H., 83, 184n.
Davidson, K., 24, 181n.
Davis, C.J., 27, 181n.
Davis, S.F., 17, 26, 185n., 187n.
Deaf children and drawings, 27-28
Decompensation, 38
De Martino, M.F., 29, 181n.
Dennis, W., 111, 112, 114-16, 118, 181n.
Denver Developmental Screening Test, 13
Dependency, 45, 53, 56, 63, 70
and mouths, 44

Depersonalization feelings, 45
Depression, 18, 91, 92
and color, 35
Deren, S., 78, 181n.
De Respinis, M., 39, 185n.
Derr, J., 80, 186n.
Diaz-Guerrero, R., 117, 183n.
Dickson, J.D., 37, 187n.
Di Leo, J.H., v-vi, 18, 79, 181n.
Dillard, H.K., 19, 181n.
Dissociation in drawings, 22-23
Dodds, J.B., 14, 181n.
Draw-a-Car Test, 39
Draw-a-Classroom (DAC) Test, 85
Draw-a-Family (DAF) Test, 77-79, 85
Draw-a-Group (DAG) Test, 82, 85
Draw-a-Man (DAM) Test, v, 13, 115.
   See also Draw-a-Person Test
Draw-a-Person (DAP) Test, 17-49, 87
   and age changes, 33
   Draw-a-Person-in-the-Rain Test, 38-39
   Inside-of-the-Body Test, 39, 40, 41
   instructions for administration of, 41
   interpretation of, 31-32, 42-46
      overall impression, 42-43
      specific signs in, 43-46
   literature on, 34
   and questions, 36
   reliability of, 30
   scoring/interpretation of, 18-20
   sexual identification on, 20-21
   validity of, 21-30
   variations of, 35-40
Draw-a-Teacher (DAT) Test, 143
Dunleavy, R.A., 13, 181n.

Ears in drawings, 44, 50, 64, 65, 67
Eisenman, R., 116, 180n.
Ekman, P., 5, 181n.
Encephalitis, 29
Engle, P.L., 19, 143, 181n.
Erasures in drawings, 46, 143
Evanston Early Identification Scale (EEIS), 19, 22
Expansiveness, 42
Eyes in drawings, 44, 64
   omission of, 19

Face:
   deceptive expressions of, 5-6
Family Relations Indicator (FRI), 80
Faterson, H.F., 33, 181n.
Feet in drawings, 60, 61, 62, 64, 68
   omission of, 19, 44
Femininity concerns, 119, 126, 134
Figure placement in drawings, 46

189

Fisher, G.M., 21, 181n.
Flannigan, M.W., 142, 187n.
Foley, J.P., 112, 116, 179n.
Forehead in drawings, 65
Fox, C., 24, 181n.
Frankenburg, W.K., 14, 181n.
Freud, S., 6
Friesen, W.V., 5, 181n.
Fuller, G.R., 29, 181n.

Gardiner, H.W., 14, 112, 115, 181n.
Gaston, D.E., 21, 186n.
Gender:
   dominance in, 117-18
   and religious content in drawings, 113
General Anxiety Scale, 24
Gesell Incomplete Man Test, 13
Gestalt of drawings, 77-78
Gestures, unconscious, 5
Goffeney, B., 117, 182n.
Goodenough, F.L., v, viin., 13, 18, 111, 113, 181n.
Grandiosity, 42, 48
Green, M., 29, 182n.
Greenberg, J.W., 83, 184n.
Greenberg, R.P., 28, 182n.
Griffith, A.V., 30, 182n.
Group values in drawings, 12-13, 111-41
   instructions for, 118
   interpretation of, 118-20
   research on, 111-18

Hair in drawings, 48, 71, 90, 113, 114, 116, 122, 124, 126, 132, 134, 139, 141
Hall, L.P., 22, 182n.
Halo effect in measurement, 10
Hammer, E.F., 18, 22, 23, 32, 35, 175, 180n., 182n.
Hammer, M., 21, 30, 33, 182n.
Handler, L., 24, 25, 39, 182n.
Hands in drawings, 22, 53, 62, 68, 145, 170, 171
   omission of, 19, 44
Handwriting, 112
Hanson, J.L., 13, 181n.
Hare, A.P., 82, 85, 182n.
Hare, R.T., 82, 85, 182n.
Harris, D.B., v, viin., 13, 14, 113, 182n.
Hawkins, W.F., 29, 181n.
Heads in drawings 18, 30, 41, 43-44, 50-53, 56, 57, 65, 67, 69, 155
Health care in drawings, 144-47, 159-73
Hearing, impaired and children, 27
Heights of figures in drawings, 82

Heinrich, P., 20, 182n.
Henderson, N.B., 117, 182n.
Henrich, L., 38, 187n.
Hiland, D.N., 24, 37, 185n.
Hiler, E.W., 32, 182n.
Hills, J., 143, 179n.
Hoopes, J.L., 27, 181n.
Hostility in drawings, 115, 120, 125, 127, 128, 138
House-Tree-Person (HTP) Test, vi, 13, 18, 23, 27, 31, 35, 37, 40
Hulse, W.C., 77, 78, 182n.
Humor-ridicule in drawings, 114, 119, 123, 135, 137, 138, 140, 143
Hutchinson, S.H., 116, 180n.

Identification of children, 142
Ilg, F.L., 13, 182n.
Impulsivity, 11
Indians, Canadian, 72, 112-41
Individuality-uniqueness in drawings, 175
Inside-of-the-Body Test, 39-40
Institute for Personality and Ability Testing (IPAT) Anxiety Scale, 24
IQ tests, v, 20, 23, 28, 31, 51, 52, 53, 55, 74, 83

Jacobson, D.A., 81, 182n.
Joesting, J., 30, 180n.
Johnson, F.A., 28, 182n.
Johnson, J.H., 23, 24, 183n.
Johnson, O.G., 28, 183n., 187n.
Jolles, I., 18, 35, 183n.

Kahn, S.B., 11, 144, 183n.
Kaimen, B.D., 20, 179n.
Kaplan, A.M., 30, 33, 182n.
Kaplan, W., 21, 182n.
Katzaroff, M.D., v, viin.
Kaufman, S.H., vi, viin., 79-81, 85, 88, 175, 180n.
Kerschensteiner, D.G., vi, viin.
Kinetic Family Drawings (KFD) Test, 79-83, 85, 175
Kinetic School Drawing (KSD) Test, 82-83
Kirchner, J.H., 36, 184n.
Klepsch, M.E., vi, xi, xii, 30, 113, 114, 116, 143, 144, 145, 147, 176, 183n.
Klopfer, W.G., 34, 183n.
Koch's Baumtest, vi
Koff, E., 21, 185n.
Koppitz, E.M., vi, viin., 13, 18, 19, 21, 22, 23, 25, 29, 45, 79, 183n.

190

191

Thurber, S., 113, 186n.
Tolor, A., 20, 32, 186n.
Tolor, B., 20, 186n.
Tomblen, D., 23, 185n.
Triebe, J.K., 20, 182n.
Turner, W., 6

Uhlenhuth, E.H., 82, 180n.
Uhlin, D.M., 37, 187n.
Underlining in drawings, 87-88
Uras, A., 114, 181n.
Urban, W.H., 18, 187n.

Vale, H.L., 26, 38, 181n.
Velicer, W.F., 31, 180n.
Venham, L., 19, 24, 186n.
Verbal skills, 10-11
Verinis, J.S., 38, 187n.

Wagner, R.F., 27, 187n.

Waite, R., 24, 181n.
Walter, C.L., 20, 179n.
Wanderer, Z.W., 32, 187n.
Wawrzaszek, F., 28, 183n., 187n.
Webb, E.J., 11, 187n.
Weider, A., 20, 187n.
Welch, I.D., 142, 143, 175, 187n.
Wenger, K.W., 80, 184n.
Whitmyre, J.W., 31, 187n.
Whitney, E., 28, 187n.
Wilee, C.T., 26, 187n.
Witkin, H.A., 33, 181n.
Women's Liberation Movement, 21
Writing skills, 10-11
Wysocki, A.C., 29, 187n.
Wysocki, B.A., 28, 29, 187n.

Zaba, J.N., 27, 31, 179n.
Ziv, A., 32, 187n.
Zuk, G.H., 33, 187n.